# THE MORIZO STORY
Dr. Jack Fujimoto

The life story of an immigrant from Hiroshima, Japan who came to the United States at the age of 15

FriesenPress

One Printers Way
Altona, MB R0G 0B0
Canada

www.friesenpress.com

**Copyright © 2021 by Jack Fujimoto**
First Edition — 2021

All rights reserved.

No part of this publication may be reproduced in any form, or by any means, electronic or mechanical, including photocopying, recording, or any information browsing, storage, or retrieval system, without permission in writing from FriesenPress.

ISBN
978-1-03-912208-6 (Hardcover)
978-1-03-912207-9 (Paperback)
978-1-03-912209-3 (eBook)

1. BIOGRAPHY & AUTOBIOGRAPHY, CULTURAL HERITAGE, ASIAN & ASIAN AMERICAN

Distributed to the trade by The Ingram Book Company

# THE MORIZO STORY
## （冨士本守三）

The life story of an immigrant from Hiroshima, Japan
who came to the United States at the age of 15

## JACK FUJIMOTO, Ph.D.

Dedicated to Emi, his wife of sixty-two years

And the siblings of their marriage.

(Left to right)

Yoko, Fumie, Mother Emi Annie, Jack Masakazu,

Father Morizo, Takashi, Judy Fujie, Eiko Kay

# FUJIMOTO FAMILY TREE

|  |  |
|---|---|
| **Tameshiro** | **Fumi** |
| 1841-1912 | 1841-1911 |
| (71 years) | (70 years) |

| Motoshiro | Yasukichi | Rai | Sayo |
|---|---|---|---|
| (Yasukichi's brother) | 1868-1956 (89 years) | 1869-1926 (57 years) | (Yasukichi's second wife) |

## Yasukichi and Rai Fujimoto Family

**TATSUNO**
1888 - ?
Married Tajima
Daughter Yoshiye

**SHIZUNO**
1890 - 1957
Divorced Imada, Zentaro
Married Okabeppu, Toragesa
Sons Itaru, Hayato, Akira, Takeshi
Daughters Toshiko, Meriko

**SAYO**
1893 - ?
Divorced Takaoka, Zentaro
Married Utada, Yoshitaka
Sons Yoshihide, Yoshihiko
Daughters Tomiko, Teruko

**YUTAKA**
1896 - 1947
Married Shindo, Hisayo
Son Akiyoshi Archie
Daughters Akiko Ann, Sumiko, Yukie, Seiko

**YAYA**
1898 - ?
Married Okabeppu, Ginzo

**KISANO**
1900 - ?
Married Murakami, Mataichi
Son Choji

**MORIZO**
1902 - 1994
Married Emi Yoneda
Sons Mazakazu Jack, Takashi Thomas
Daughters Fumie, Yoko, Fujie Judy, Eiko Kay

**SAYOKO**
1904 - 1907

**YASUKO**
1906 - ?
Married Sakai
Divorced

# MILESTONES

**1902:** Morizo was one of nine children born to Yasukichi and Rai Fujimoto in Shiwa, Hiroshima-ken, Japan, on February 8.

**1915:** Morizo attended Shiwa Elementary School through the eighth grade.

**1917:** Morizo immigrated to the United States through San Francisco's Angel Island to join his father, Yasukichi, and older brother, Yutaka.

**1917 to 1927:** Ages fifteen through twenty-five, spent years in California, mostly in Southern California.

**1927:** Morizo married Emi Yoneda at the Buddhist Temple of San Diego through the help of Nihei Yokoyama.

**1927:** Morizo leased farmland in Sunnyside on the outskirts of San Diego to grow vegetable crops and raise a family of three children.

**1937:** Morizo leased farmland in Encinitas adjacent to older brother, Yutaka's farm, to grow truck vegetable crops. Two children were added to family.

**1942:** Morizo took family to Poston Concentration Camp in Arizona to comply with World War II military directive.

**1945:** Morizo, with twenty-five dollars in hand, took his family back to Encinitas upon conclusion of World War II and sharecropped with Eugene Ben Vau. One additional child was added to the family, making total of six children.

**1948:** Morizo bought real property in southern part of Encinitas using his son's name to make the purchase and grew vegetable crops and later, grew flowers.

**1967:** Morizo and Emi retired from farming.

**1989:** Morizo lost Emi.

**1994:** Morizo passed away.

# INTRODUCTION

Who was Morizo Fujimoto? He was my father.

Morizo, now in Amida's Pure Land (Buddhist term) and hearing what he said through one of his counselors, "Forgive me for treating you the way that I did because that is all I knew to raise you and the rest of the family." Tam Matsumoto, my niece who lives in Encinitas, California, is my clairvoyant interpreter who communicates with Morizo and Emi, her grandparents, and tells me what they are saying and doing in their world. How fascinating to hear what Tam tells me, and at times, read her colorful interpretation of messages.

In 2020, in the midst of the global pandemic of COVID-19, Tam wrote to Maya, our youngest daughter, that Emi (Tam's grandmother and my mother) was watching me as a butterfly. Sure enough, more recently, I have been seeing more butterflies floating by in my backyard. Indeed, this is an interesting observation.

One message from Morizo, as interpreted by Tam, had to do with his treatment of me as a youngster when I was taken to the woodshed to sit, never a physical beating.

From Morizo, I have learned much, inherited much, and adapted to his teachings. I am grateful.

It is to that end that I have written this biography of Morizo.

# SOME SHORTCOMINGS

The early days in living as the oldest son of Morizo is written much more in depth than my writings in later stages of life when we lived apart and experienced less common ground.

I have tried to paint Morizo's roots based on visiting his ancestral roots, his *furusato* (ancestral homestead), in Hiroshima, Japan, as well as his days in America. Original documents were difficult to obtain. Visits to his village registry did not produce early day family history much of it due to World War II. Many gaps exist in trying to capture his life. So, to that end, I regret that I could not capture more of his rich life.

It is with a deep sense of gratitude that I write this short biographical sketch of a man who taught me much about life and how to live it: some from his personal values, some from his activities, and some from what he cherished.

In the end, what Morizo cherished the most was his family, streams of children, grandchildren, and great-grandchildren came to visit him and Emi Annie Yoneda Fujimoto.

## VALUES

Having spent seventy-seven of his ninety-two years outside of his native Japan, he still retained much of the traditional Japanese values and traits that defined himself as a product of two cultures, Japanese and American.

Since he favored much of the Japanese values, his urge to learn English was not a priority and so, later in life, he still conversed at home in Japanese.

*Tatemae* (建前) and *Honne* (本音) come to mind. So do other well-known and storied values such as *Giri* (義理), *Ninjo* (人情), *Gimu* (義務), *Enryo* ( 遠慮 ), *Mottai Nai* (もったいない) are other values that Morizo taught me. As the narrative of Morizo's life unfolds, these values will blossom.

## TAKE NO DEBT

Morizo had a personal policy of not being obligated to others, especially taking on debt. Being a farmer and community-minded person in a small Japanese ethnic population made it difficult to avoid debt.

But, in general, Morizo was a frugal man, and so, as kids, we were denied many necessities as our neighbors.

Fortunately, we were befriended by many good people. Despite the overriding mood in farming that was resentful to Japanese farmers, it gave us, the young, opportunities that the poor could study and turn to our benefit.

## WORK ETHIC

Morizo had a strong work ethic. As his oldest son, I often got delegated to tend to the farm. Even as a young boy, Morizo instilled in me that attitude, "Work hard every day and you will be rewarded." How? When? "Make the best of every opportunity."

## SPIRITUAL MAN

Morizo was close to the Buddhist Temple of San Diego. He and Reverend Nishii often held activities at the temple for the Japanese immigrants. Morizo was the first president of the Young Men's Buddhist Association (YMBA) in 1929.

In a way, Morizo was following in the footsteps of his father, Yasukichi Fujimoto, who had a large *Butsudan* (仏壇) in his Hiroshima home, even during our frequent visits to the *furusato* (故郷) (homestead).

## LEADERSHIP

Morizo was more inclined to work with others in a leadership capacity. His style was less individualistic but embodied more of a group culture where he relied on the work and cooperation of a group of people.

He often uttered the words, "*okagesama de*," meaning that it is in the shadow of many that he accomplished what he wanted. Throughout this biographical narrative of Morizo, his leadership will emerge as a strong point in his life.

## GRATITUDE

So, with much gratitude, I appreciated the guidance given by Morizo in our early years and especially, liberating me from following in his farming enterprise. I knew my future was not in farming.

Jack Fujimoto

## OBLIGATION

It is my obligation to portray Morizo as I knew him in the following pages with accuracy. Where I fall short with errors or misinterpretations, I take responsibility.

Jack Fujimoto, Ph.D.

*Map of Hiroshima in Japan. Small Shiwa-cho village is shown in approximate location.*

# MORIZO AND YUTAKA

It was interesting to note that Yasukichi let his two sons, Yutaka, the older one, and Morizo stay in America while all of the daughters stayed in Japan. Much of the Yasukichi Fujimoto patriarch legacy is carried in the life of Yutaka and Morizo. After all, Yasukichi was a colorful man, vagabonding to Australia for a short time, returning to Japan to father children, leaving for work in California, returning to Japan to father more children with wife, Rai, and leaving for America to work and then, return to the old homestead to father his last group of children with Rai.

Yutaka and Morizo came to America and stayed there much of their life. Unlike Yasukichi, the father, they found life difficult amidst conflicting laws, regulations, and discriminatory practices, but were able to survive, even though it was a life of poverty.

Morizo and his older brother, Yutaka, were close but with quite different skills, talents, and interests; however, they supported each other in their unique ways.

In their earlier years in America, it was not clear that they intended to return to Hiroshima to live with their treasure chest as many Issei (first generation immigrants) wanted to do; however, with their large families, it became clearer that they wanted to live in America.

When Morizo became a naturalized citizen of the United States of America in 1954, it was much more definitive that he was American and no longer a Japanese citizen. Many Japanese retained their Japanese citizenship along with their American citizenship, but not Morizo.

So, in his later forty years of life, Morizo probably took no more than five trips to Japan, indicating his detachment and pursuing his establishment of American roots.

## RETURN TO VISIT JAPAN

One trip was to develop the Fujimoto headstone in the family cemetery as a permanent resting place for him and his successor generations. (代々の墓).

Morizo's older brother, Yutaka, died tragically from an accident in 1947; therefore, Morizo became heir apparent to protect the Shiwa（志和）homestead.

## ADOPTING A SON

So, he took another trip to adopt Hirotoshi Murakami as a son to care for the Fujimoto homestead, but when Hirotoshi abdicated, Morizo went again, this time to adopt Hirotoshi's brother to become the legal owner of the Fujimoto homestead. Kyohei became Morizo's adopted son. This type of adoption, for legal reasons, was less common than the adoption for surnames so that family lineage can be retained.

To simplify matters, as Morizo's oldest son, I could have volunteered to take over the Shiwa homestead but that was not my choice.

On another visit, I believe Morizo went to see the Okabeppu brothers in Kagoshima as well as the Osaka World's Fair. All in all, Morizo was not a frequent visitor to Japan. Grace and I went more than thirty times to Japan, far more than Morizo.

## SOME CLARIFICATION FOR STORY

The first part of *The Morizo Story* starts with some controversial interpretations that I wish to clarify. This part may be unique to me, but if followed according to popular usage might have affected Morizo's life as well as my life tremendously.

## FIRST CONTROVERSY

The first controversy has to do with the English translation of Japanese sounds or phonemes where the Western adoption of the Hepburn system causes some irregular English wording. My example is that "Huzi" is a proper writing for "Fuji" (ふじ) that is more commonly accepted in the English language.

## SECOND CONTROVERSY

The second controversy that I discuss are the Chinese characters that are used for "Fujimoto." Why is our Chinese character used in "Fujimoto" so much different from the regularly used one in Japanese writings? The more common "Fujimoto" is written in Japanese as 藤本 whereas our *furusato* name is written 冨士本. Another way of "Fujimoto" that I have seen is 不二本.

## ANOTHER CONTROVERSY

There is also the superstition surrounding the number of strokes used in names such as mine where Masakazu is written with one set of Chinese characters (正和) but later in life, Morizo changed it to ( 真上 ) due to the number of strokes in writing it was a bad omen. I do not understand this aspect of interpretation, but I can sense it when I was told not to get married in September (*kugatsu*) (九月) because *ku* is *nine* but also interpreted as *kuroo*（苦労）

which can be *hard work* throughout my married life. Similarly, for April (*shigatsu*) (四月) where *shi* (死) can be a symbol for *death* which can denote dying . . . same reading but different interpretation. Such superstitions or interpretations are found throughout Japanese thought.

Despite all of my hang-ups in writing this biography of Morizo, I have approached it mainly from a chronological perspective. The reader will note that a more general approach is used as opposed to many specifics. I talk about Morizo's many experiences intertwined with much of his brother, Yutaka's experiences, and in many cases, with my experiences.

Despite lack of documentation from official city hall records because many were lost during World War II as well as interpretations from documents that I found among Morizo's records, this biography is filled with love for my father (and also my mother).

# FUJI (ふじ) OR HUZI (ふじ)

How much could my life have changed if the Japanese characters were written using a scientific method of writing the English alphabet instead of the commonly used Hepburn system of Romanization?

Fuji would have been written Huzi!!!

If my identity was Jack Huzimoto rather than Jack Fujimoto, my seat in elementary school would be with the *H* group rather than the *F* group.

This was a sticking point with me because the teacher seated us often in alphabetical order with me sitting next to a short, pudgy, smelly student named "Folkes" rather than with "Hunt," a cute blonde student who was often smiling at me. Identity was important.

The scientific as well as the Hepburn classification of Japanese Romanization would start with the vowels: *a*, *i*, *u*, *e*, and *o*.

By observing the two methods of Romanizing the Japanese hiragana, the popular method uses the Hepburn system; however, was the literary world advanced through the Hepburn system that focused on the sound of the Japanese word?

Not for me!

# FUJIMOTO (藤本) OR FUJIMOTO (冨士本)

The Fujimoto homestead in rural Hiroshima, Japan, has property that includes rice-growing paddies, vegetable gardens, fruit trees, a large pond, as well as a family cemetery on the side of a mountain owned by the family for many years.

We have visited the homestead and the family cemetery on numerous occasions.

One of the headstones in the family cemetery is small but engraved with "Fujimoto Ya" (藤本屋) showing *Bunka Roku Nen*. The largest headstone in this private cemetery shows "Fujimoto Ke" (冨士本家). The *kanji* (Chinese character) for "Fuji" in both headstones are different.

*This headstone shows "Fujimoto Ya."*

*This headstone shows "Bunka Roku Nen" and "Bunka Shichi Nen" which signifies the "Sixth and Seventh Year" of the "Bunka" era.*

*This headstone is engraved with "Namu Amida Butsu" and has "Fujimoto Ke" below it. Below that is the marble gate which, when lifted, will accept any urn with ashes of future Fujimoto clan members. I am standing next to the headstone.*

## WHY?

My guess is that the Fujimoto homestead was designated with the "Ya" character because it served as an administrative unit in the governing of the Shiwa region in rural Hiroshima during the 1800s when the Tokugawa shogunate relied on such homesteads to collect taxes in the form of bushels of rice, as well as serving the Japanese shogun government as a stopping off point . . . room and board. That is the reason for the "Ya" appended to Fujimoto in the cemetery.

The backside of the headstone showed its date as being in the 1830s era, which tells me that the homestead ceased being a governmental administrative unit before the end of the Tokugawa shogunate. The shogunate ceded governmental control to the Japanese emperor system in 1867, when Emperor Meiji was inaugurated.

The "Ke" designation indicated the homestead as being a family generational cemetery. There is not only the Morizo Fujimoto family designation, but also the headstones of his siblings and their families, as well as some of his cousins and their families.

And, when we observe the "Fuji" calligraphy, the *kanji* (Chinese writing) is different.

For "Fujimoto Ya," the *kanji* is the "Fuji" (藤) that is typically translated as "wisteria," a flowering tree with bright purple flowers.

The Morizo Fujimoto headstone has the "Fuji" written similar to the *kanji* used for Mount Fuji, (富士山) Japan's sacred national treasure. The family name of "Fuji" is written (冨士). Notice that the "Fu" does not have the hook on top. For whatever reason, the hook is missing.

So, when we trace the Morizo ancestry, we can safely say that the Fujimoto homestead served an important position in rural Shiwa, Hiroshima, Japan. It is then, no wonder, that my visits to the *furusato* (roots) resulted in neighbors saying that the Fujimoto homestead was the "mayor's house."

# THE YASUKICHI (保吉) FUJIMOTO FAMILY

The Fujimoto Ya headstone in the family gravesite in the mountain behind the Fujimoto homestead showed that the Fujimoto family shed its governmental administrative work in the 1830s.

*The Morizo Story* starts with his grandparents, Tameshiro and Fumi. Living through seventy years of age in Shiwa, Hiroshima, Japan, they lived quite lengthy lives. They were farmers.

Having been born in 1841, and no longer involved in the governance of Shiwa area, they were still privileged in a society that listed the daimyo and samurai in its top rung, followed by farmers and the artisans. It was somewhat similar to a caste system where the lord and his cadre were the rulers.

The farmers produced the rice that was the basis of taxation to support and sustain the samurai class.

## TAMESHIRO AND FUMI FUJIMOTO

Tameshiro and Fumi Fujimoto had two sons, Motoshiro and Yasukichi, the latter being the father of Morizo. Motoshiro was the older son but abdicated that significant position because, as I heard from my cousin, Yoshiye Tajima, Motoshiro and his wife told Tameshiro that they would not take responsibility for the "mayor's house."

So, in essence, Tameshiro reasoned that Yasukichi and Rai would be more responsible and therefore, be the caretaker of the *honke* (the main house operator) of the Shiwa *furusato* or thatch-roofed home. To this day, Yasukichi and his lineage have occupied the main house.

It is interesting to note that our family did not settle for common names typically found among families such as "Ichiro," "jiro," "saburo," for first son, second son, and third son. Or, females might be "kazue" or "kazuko" ending with "e" or "ko." Where did Yasukichi and Rai come to name my father, Morizo? It is somewhat out of character because it has "three" in the name but lacks any "three" as a reference point. I can only surmise that there may have been another son before my father, which would make sense because, then, my father would be the third son to "protect" the homestead. Anyway, just curious.

I could make the same argument for Yutaka, Morizo's brother.

## YASUKICHI AND RAI

Yasukichi was born in 1868 and Rai in 1869, just after the Tokugawa shogunate had turned over their reins to the newly crowned Emperor Meiji. The Meiji era in Japanese history was significant in that the Western powers opened the doors of Japan to foreign countries. This Meiji reformation resulted in Japanese being sent to many foreign lands to learn Western ways. Transportation and communication became an area of keen interest along with the currency system and banking enterprises. It was the unmasking of an insular Japan to Western ways. It was in that kind of environment that Yasukichi was born.

Yasukichi and Rai raised a family of nine children: seven daughters and two sons. Yasukichi had a sizable farm including a mountain. This property is what we visited often in our visits to Japan.

Yasukichi was the unsaid "mayor's office." With this, there were certain protocols and responsibilities. He was a busy man who seemed to be caught up in the outward push of the Meiji government, and at the same time, mindful of his farm and family.

## YASUKICHI, THE PATRIARCH

*Pictured are Yasukichi Fujimoto, seated, and Toragesa Okabeppu.*

After Emperor Meiji passed away, Emperor Taisho took the throne in 1912. It was shortly after that, Yasukichi came to the San Diego area as a farm laborer. He brought Yutaka, his first son, with him. He worked primarily in the Chula Vista area with Toragesa Okabeppu, who married Yasukichi's second daughter, Shizuno.

Shizuno had originally married and had a son, Hajime, but he expired in three days. Having had a sad tragedy, I could only surmise the Yasukichi needed a woman to care for him and Yutaka, while, at the same time, needed to be with Toragesa Okabeppu, who was single at the time. It was a rare and convenient opportunity to have Toragesa and Shizuno marry.

It was interesting to note that Shizuno was a divorcée who married Toragesa and came to Southern California. Later, I learned that Yasukichi's daughters, Sayo and Yasuko, also became divorcées. I had assumed that wives were devoted to their husbands, and therefore, divorce was unheard of, but my assumption was not correct.

*Pictured are from left to right, Yutaka, Toragesa Okabeppu, Yasukichi, and Morizo, my father.*

## YASUKICHI AND TORAGESA

Toragesa and Shizuno had four boys born in the Chula Vista area. It must have been a busy time for Yasukichi, Yutaka, Toragesa, and Shizuno, not only with their work, but also caring for the four Okabeppu boys: Itaru, Hayato, Akira, and Takeshi. The whole entourage pulled up work and returned to Japan in 1924. Toragesa and Shizuno returned to Kagoshima, while Yasukichi and Yutaka went to Hiroshima.

In the meantime, my father, Morizo, did not return to Japan, but was going to school in Los Angeles, picking up day jobs, and paying for room and board at the Hiroshima Hotel in downtown Los Angeles.

## MY ENCOUNTER WITH YASUKICHI

I met Yasukichi only one time in my life. That was in their Hiroshima farmhouse, their *furusato*. Rai had died in 1926 and Yasukichi married Sayo Kubo who had greeted me with Yasukichi in 1951.

I was an American Army serviceman, newly assigned to the 441st Counter Intelligence Detachment assigned to Tokyo in April 1950. One of my first assignments was to accompany a US military tank on a flatbed car from Camp Drake on the outskirts of Yokohama to the ANZAC headquarters in Hiro, outside of Hiroshima. The ANZAC, Australian, and New Zealand occupation forces, controlled the Hiroshima area. For me, it was an unusual assignment in that I had to run shotgun for a military tank, much less knowing anything about a tank or what I could do if it rolled.

Before getting a permanent Counter Intelligence Corps (CIC) assignment, I took time to visit Yasukichi and Sayo in rural Shiwa, traveling by bus and taxi. When arriving at the thatched-roof house about noon in my US Army uniform, Yasukichi and Sayo were eating and ignored me.

After a long few minutes, I got tired of waiting to be invited to the tatami-floored main room where they were eating. I yelled that I was his grandson from California and came to visit him. Whether he was hard of hearing or not, or his eyesight was poor, I did not know. He was in his eighties and might have. In any event,

Yasukichi apologized, saying that he ignored me because there were many black marketeers coming to his house and he ignored them . . . but me, in a military uniform!

I do not recall our conversation, but with my being a Japanese language interpreter and translator, I spoke to my grandfather in Japanese.

I learned much of my fluency in the Japanese language at home where Morizo and Emi spoke more in Japanese language than they did in the English language. They had limited command of the English language. It says much about their communications skills to survive in an alien environment where they were still Japanese citizens and not able to buy or own real property.

*This rare photograph shows Yasukichi and Sayo flanking the Buddhist priest. There is no Yutaka or Morizo in this photograph, only their sisters. Back row shows Morizo's older sister, Kisano, on the left. She is the only sister pictured whom I met when visiting Hiroshima.*

One incident that I recall when visiting Yasukichi and Sayo involved his putting me to work in his vegetable garden. I was given a bucket, scooped the "honey" from the toilet basin (you pooped down a straight pipe to a basin), and took a dipper to spread the "honey" to the vegetables. Japan-grown vegetables, for this reason, was off-limits to GIs.

In the city, the "honey scoopers" were large trucks with tanks storing the "honey."

Yasukichi lived a long life, passing away at the age of eighty-nine, in 1956.

*Pictured is Yasukichi at the family cemetery that is carved out of the mountainside. The mountain is owned by Yasukichi. There were several family cemeteries, but the Yasukichi-owned one was the only one where headstones were placed on multiple levels of the cemetery.*

For me, it was a memorable moment having met Yasukichi once. I appreciated his being frank with me when I visited him in 1950. My one regret is that I could not find a photograph of Rai, who mothered my father, Morizo.

# YASUKICHI, A SPIRITUAL MAN

When Grace and I visit the old homestead in Shiwa (Hiroshima-ken), we are relegated to sleeping in the old straw-thatched roof house that has the Buddhist altar in the room along with its many adornments on the sliding doors or hanging in the room. When we get ready to retire, we close the altar.

It is amazing that such a beautiful Buddhist altar is still maintained in the old house. All of the gold-covered adornments along with pictures and holders covered in gold is a sight to see. To maintain this altar in such wonderful condition is a fine testimonial to Nobuko who now occupies the farmhouse.

The gold-plated ornaments in the altar are costly. Recently, the altar for the West Los Angeles Buddhist Temple where Grace and

I attend and which is much larger than pictured here, was refurbished with gold plating by a professional group from Japan. The temple raised nearly half a million dollars to pay for the work.

I can only surmise that Yasukichi maintained the pictured altar during his years living in the Fujimoto homestead.

Further evidence of Yasukichi valuing his spirit is captured in some of the writings posted to the sliding doors to the room as well as the walls.

Above the altar is a framed calligraphy showing "absolute truth."

Below in the altar is a figurine of the Buddha defined in gold. It was probably in this type of milieu that Morizo learned from Yasukichi about spiritual values captured through the Amida Buddha and chanting, "*Namo Amida Butsu*." It is not a prayer or petition but to signify that Yasukichi and later, Morizo, believed in the Buddha and his Dharma.

The Morizo Story

*Pictured is a sliding door with Japanese calligraphy written on it.*

As a teenager, I heard Morizo often talk about philosophy and absolutes expressed in the Buddha's teachings, such as "interdependency," "change is constant," "compassion and wisdom," as well as "*giri ninjo.*"

I do not know what it says; however, all of the sliding doors to the altar had writings or pictures. For these to survive the test of time only tells me that the woman of the house had them well preserved.

*Some of the writings were preserved on portable screens as pictured here.*

Even though I served as an interpreter-translator of the Japanese language while in the American military forces, I do not know what is said on these screens.

*Beautiful black-and-white painting on one of the screens.*

All in all, I believe that Morizo learned much from Yasukichi about the spiritual side of life and living. Morizo never preached to me about being a Buddhist, but only that, I should seek out what I believe.

To this day, I have valued and treasured what I learned and have lived a life of following the Buddha's path.

# YASUKICHI AND RAI

Yasukichi and Rai were married in 1887. They had a large family, nine kids in all.
Tazuno was born in 1888.
Shizuno was born in 1890.
Sayo was born in 1893.
Yutaka, son, was born in 1896.
Yaya was born in 1898.
Kisano was born in 1900.
Morizo, my father, was born in 1902.
Sayoko was born in 1904.
Yasuko was born in 1906.
Yasukichi died in 1956 at the age of eight-nine in Shiwa, Hiroshima, while two sons were in America. Yutaka predeceased him in 1947 in a La Jolla, California, hospital after a terrible accident.
Rai died in 1926 at the age of fifty-seven after giving birth to a large family.
Yasukichi then married Sayo Kubo but had no children.

# YASUKICHI AND TORAGESA

At the advent of World War I in 1914, Yasukichi (保吉) and Yutaka（行）, his first son, along with Toragesa Okabeppu and his wife, Shizuno, (Yasukichi's second daughter and a divorcée) were in the Chula Vista area of San Diego County.

*Pictured are Okabeppu, Toragesa and Shizuno on left side and Yutaka and Hisayo on the right side.*

Toragesa was from Kagoshima, located in the southern part of Kyushu.

They were probably farm laborers in the celery production and distribution market. I learned from an exhibit in the Chula Vista Museum that the hybrid white celery became a "big hit" with markets in America's East Coast and so, production soared and laborers were needed.

I learned later from Xavier del Buono, an academic colleague of mine, that his father told him about the high profits from celery crops in the Chula Vista area and so, in 1920 or 1921, a strike took place for higher wages and better working conditions. Xavier's father was one of the strike leaders.

Toragesa Okabeppu and Shizuno started their family of four boys there.

Itaru was born in 1918.
Hayato was born in 1920.
Akira was born in 1922.
Takeshi was born in 1924.

*Pictured is a 2006 photograph of Hayato, Akira, Jack (author), and Takeshi in the Kagoshima home of Hayato. The oldest brother, Itaru, is not in the picture.*

As an aside, it is believed that Itaru passed away in the Stockton area of California and did not return to his family's Kagoshima roots. I checked several offices in Stockton and San Joaquin Valley but could not locate any death certificate for Itaru Okabeppu. When the Okabeppu family had a fiftieth anniversary memorial service, they asked me to get a statement from the Stockton Medical Clinic showing that he had been treated there, but no further information was available.

## RETURN TO JAPAN

Yasukichi and Yutaka, along with Toragesa and his family, returned to Hiroshima and Kagoshima respectively in 1924, the year of the Japanese Exclusion Act in California.

Okabeppu, Toregesa, and wife, Shizuno, took Akira and Takeshi to Kagoshima *furusato* (roots), leaving Itaru and Hayato to go with Yasukichi and Yutaka to Shiwa in Hiroshima where they went to Shiwa Elementary School. This was the same school that my father, Morizo, had attended.

Later, Toragesa and Shizuno added two daughters, Toshiko and Meriko, after returning to Kagoshima. Toshiko married in Kagoshima and lived close to the Okabeppu homestead. Meriko married a Catholic in Yamanashi near Tokyo and had a large family of ten kids. All in all, one could surmise that the Fujimoto offspring were many.

Yutaka married Hisayo Shindo in 1925 at their *furusato* in their Shiwa homestead.

In the meantime, my father, Morizo, was in California from 1917 and remained here when his father and brother returned to Japan.

# MORIZO, EARLY DAYS

Morizo, my father, was born in Shiwa (village), Hiroshima, Japan, on February 8, 1902.

*Pictured is the century-old straw-thatched-roof house that was expanded with the building of a two-story living quarters by Morizo's adopted son, Kyohei and Nobuko, for their four boys. I took the photograph in 2006 on a visit to Shiwa. Behind the thatched-roof house was the warehouse and equipment storage space. Kyohei and Nobuko later ceded part of their property to Yoshiye Tajima, daughter of Morizo's oldest sister. Morizo had directed that they do so and register the transaction with the village office.*

Shiwa is in Kamo-gun, the home base of the famous KamoTsuru, Japanese rice wine. So, when I mention KamoTsuru, most Japanese know the location of Shiwa.

Morizo was born in the above straw-thatched-roof house that has historic roots. During and after the civil war in Japan, *sengoku jidai,* of the late 1400s and early 1500s, the Hiroshima area was ruled by the Lord Mori, Akinori and his samurai. The farmers and merchants supported the daimyo or lord through their production of rice, vegetables, and fruits of daily living, as well as supported the service industries, the carpenters, shopkeepers, and others. The reward meted out by the clan lord was usually through the distribution of rice. So, when the lord awarded one of his samurai, it was usually barked out as "100 *koku*" for example meaning that the samurai was given an additional 100 bushels of rice. That rice was produced by farmers and paid as tax to the lord's coffers.

The Shiwa household that Grace and I often visited is about 140 years old, with some improvements made recently. Kyohei, our adopted brother, and his family, added rooms, changed the roof from straw thatched to tile, but kept the storage shed and warehouse intact with straw matting and roofing. This is the same house that served the government in the Shiwa area.

With six siblings before him, Morizo probably did not get much attention. He attended the local Shiwa Elementary School.

When Morizo enrolled in Shiwa Elementary School, the Japanese nation had fought and was victorious over the Russian fleet in their 1906 war, the first time that an Asian nation had defeated a European power. Admiral Heihachiro Togo had established himself as a "brilliant" naval officer and gave the Japanese nation some sense of becoming a world nation to be watched. In fact, history shows that Japan became an ally of European nations during World War I and occupied the many territories of the defeated German Republic of World War I.

Morizo showed me a picture of his graduating elementary school class with names attached. This, to me, indicated that he had a good mind to recall his classmates. Morizo graduated from Shiwa Elementary School in 1914 when Japan was wrapped in euphoria first with Admiral Togo's naval victory and later, when the army started to "stretch its influence."

With World War I, Japan sided with the Allies (Great Britain, America, and others) to oppose Germany. Like Morizo said one day, Emperor Taisho rode a white horse to show the military might of Japan. So, even Morizo thought that the cavalry might be a good fit.

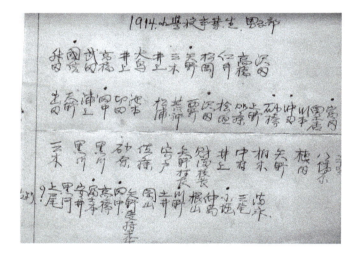

*Morizo lists himself as fifth from left in first row as depicted in the above picture.*

## MORIZO AT HOME

Among all of his siblings of mostly sisters from 1902, his birth date, to 1917, when he migrated to California, he probably bore the brunt of farm work on the Shiwa properties that Yasukichi owned, including the mountainside cemetery and large pond where Morizo talked fondly about learning to swim. So, being the younger son, he probably had to tend to planting and harvesting rice, grow vegetables for the house meals, and keep fruit trees producing. Also, having to tend the mountainside pines where the *matsutake* (mushrooms) grew. These mushrooms are a delicacy in Japanese cuisine.

## WHERE IS MORIZO'S FUTURE?

*Pictured is Morizo in back row, second from left, in uniform.*

At times when he later grew and harvested vegetables for the San Diego produce market from Sunnyside in the outskirts of San Diego, he would tell me about some of his earlier thoughts . . . that he did not care for the tradition of bowing his head when the emperor of Japan passed by, that he liked the white horse that the emperor rode, that he might like to join the Japanese military cavalry as a career, but was unsure about his future.

I understood that Morizo did not have the opportunity to take the military entrance examination or ride a horse because Yasukichi said that he wanted Morizo to come to San Francisco and eventually join the Okabeppu brothers and Yutaka as laborers in the suburbs of San Diego.

He also talked about his interest in Buddhism, about his spirituality, his interest in religious practices, and work with the temples.

## ELEMENTARY SCHOOL MATES

At times, Morizo talked about some of his elementary school schoolmates. Among those mentioned were Naoto Mito, a neighbor next to the Shiwa house. Naoto's son came to Los Angeles and became a sales representative for Japan Foods Corporation. Morizo saw the son several times, but not Naoto, except the one time that Morizo returned to Japan to negotiate a successor son to take over the Shiwa properties.

Another neighbor in Shiwa was the Tanaka family. Their daughter, Masaye, came to Los Angeles, got married, and presently resides in Little Tokyo Towers in downtown Los Angeles.

Another classmate was Kazuo Yano. Yano moved to Los Angeles and established the highly profitable Yano Crate Company. He sold vegetable containers to local farmers. Today, pallets are used more frequently to move boxes or containers of local fruit and vegetables. Morizo saw the Yano relatives occasionally in Los Angeles.

## MORIZO'S KARMA

Morizo commented on one occasion that had he remained in Japan after graduating from Shiwa Elementary School, he might have been conscripted for the Japanese military. The Emperor Taisho era from 1912 to 1925 was a period growing militarization.

Because Japan was becoming recognized as a world power, its military power was showing. Its naval fleet was being compared to that of the United States and Great Britain.

With the end of World War I and the formation of the League of Nations, the world powers negotiated the strength of military arsenals. Japan occupied the East Asia possessions of the defeated German Republic. But, its naval fleet was negotiated to be less than the United States or Great Britain.

This eventually led to Japan flexing its "muscle" in such a way that resulted in the occupation of Manchuria. When Emperor Hirohito took the throne in 1925, Japan was well on its way to becoming a world military power.

If Morizo had been drafted for the military at age fifteen, he might have become a cavalryman.

How things changed by Morizo being in California rather than in Japan's military force. And who knows my Karma? Having a sense of his various travels and travails leaves me with gratification that I had been able to follow my area of interest, education, with some preparation rather than the farm life that Morizo had to endure without much learning of its intricacies: the weather, the seeds, its nurturing, and producing crops be it vegetables or flowers. Also, the intricacies of financing crop production . . . no GPS or AI at that time.

# MORIZO ARRIVES IN CALIFORNIA, 1917

In 1917, at the age of fifteen, Morizo said that his mother, Rai, saw him board the large ship in Kobe, Japan, to make the long journey to join Yasukichi and Yutaka in San Francisco. When he arrived at Angel Island in San Francisco Bay, Yasukichi and Yutaka greeted him openly but soon disappeared saying that he needed to find work to support himself . . . which he did through working the grape vineyards in the Central Valley and citrus groves around Los Angeles, and eventually joining Yasukichi and Yutaka in the South Bay celery fields.

Yasukichi and Yutaka were probably quite valuable to the celery growth, harvest, and shipping operation because Yasukichi had cooking skills from his days working the railroads in and around Sacramento. Yutaka had mechanical skills.

*This 1922 photograph shows Morizo guiding a cart, place unknown.*

Before the Japanese Exclusion Act of 1924, Yasukichi, Yutaka, along with the Toragesa Okabeppu family of Shizuno and the four boys returned to Japan.

Morizo was left to fend for himself rather going back with Yasukichi and his older brother, Yutaka. It seemed fairly natural that Morizo head north to Los Angeles.

Morizo talked about his days in Los Angeles where he stayed at the Hiroshima Hotel (広島屋) in the Little Tokyo area. He attended the Frank Wiggins Trade School (now Los Angeles Trade Technical College) where he studied diesel and large engines for which he graduated with a diploma. The curriculum was in automotive engineering as listed on his diploma. The diploma was issued on September 1, 1924. To me, it is amazing that Morizo, with his limited command of the English language, could complete such a training program.

In hindsight, I did not recall that Morizo worked on such engines except that he might have done some work on his Ford-Ferguson or Massey Ferguson type of tractors on his Sunnyside farm and later, on his Encinitas farm.

Also, it was just as well that he stayed in the Los Angeles area inasmuch as some of his previously described schoolmates and their friends from Shiwa lived in Los Angeles or its suburbs. Mito and Yano continued to visit Morizo during this period and throughout the years later.

Being a bachelor and living in Little Tokyo in metropolitan Los Angeles must have provided much time for Morizo's learning of life and living in this predominantly diverse community. Nishi Hongwanji Buddhist Temple was around the corner from the Hiroshima Hotel. Noted actor, Sessue Hayakawa was becoming featured as an actor on the "silent" screen. I heard much from Sessue's son about his father becoming famous in Little Tokyo in the 1920s.

Morizo stated at one time that he worked in many citrus groves as well as farms in the Los Angeles, Orange, and San Diego counties. Maybe that is the reason for his taking up farming and a new bride, Emi Yoneda, in 1927, a year after Yutaka returned from Japan with his new bride, Hisayo Shindo.

## BIG BROTHER, YUTAKA

Yutaka returned to Shiwa with Yasukichi. Coming from a "rich" family with a legacy, Yutaka was a "most" eligible bachelor.

In 1925, Yutaka wed Shindo, Hisayo.

The Shindo family lived in poverty because of considerable debt accumulated by Hisayo's father. This was noted in a recent biography of the noted film industry "biggie," Shindo, Kaneto, Hisayo's younger brother. The wedding was a big affair according to some folks I talked to on my many visits to the Fujimoto homestead. Some folks in Shiwa continued to talk about the wedding, how it lit up the Shiwa sky. Also, the 100-year-old fir trees at the entrance to the Fujimoto household were planted in 1925 in commemoration of the wedding. After all, Yasukichi was a successful, well-heeled leader in Shiwa and needed to show his community that his first son got married.

*1924 photograph of leaders at the Buddhist Temple of San Diego. Morizo is in back row, second from right.*
*Rev. Nishii is in center of back row.*
*Morizo's good friend Zembei Iwashita is in back row, second from left.*

For my father, Morizo, there was not the same type of community fanfare in San Diego as for Yutaka in Shiwa, their *furusato* (roots). Morizo spent time at the Buddhist Temple of San Diego (BTSD).

## YUTAKA AND HISAYO SHINDO

I learned later that Yutaka and Hisayo returned to California in the Logan Heights area of San Diego and took up the growing of vegetables that they trucked to the large San Diego produce market. Yutaka was quite prosperous, not only from his farmland but also from his skills as a carpenter, craftsman, and electrical work. Also,

I learned that Yutaka sent funds to the Shindo family to ease their debt situation in Hiroshima rather than sending any funds to Yasukichi. That may have been one reason for Morizo building the Fujimoto "dai" headstone for the Fujimoto generations rather than Yutaka, who, as oldest son, with an obligation, could have been responsible for it being built on the mountainside.

After Yutaka's return to San Diego, Morizo kept in close contact with his older brother, even though they lived miles apart from each other. Since Morizo was close in his relationship with Yutaka, I think that it was natural for me to visit and become close to Yutaka's son, Akiyoshi (Archie).

A close relationship between the two brothers and their families existed until Yutaka died in an accident in 1947 (age fifty-three) and Archie died in 1996 (age seventy) while Morizo lived to 1994.

# MORIZO WEDS EMI YONEDA-1927

## EMI ANNIE YONEDA

*Pictured are Emi and Hozumi in their later years. Emi is the older sister.*

Emi and Hozumi Yoneda, sisters, returned to California in 1926 with Narumi Yoneda, their cousin, to live at the Nihei Yokoyama home in Monrovia. Nihei's wife was Hiroyo Yoneda, the older sister of Emi's father. So, Nihei had an obligation to welcome the sisters.

Narumi, the cousin, left shortly to go elsewhere in Hollywood for a board and care situation and where he could attend adult school to learn English.

## NIHEI AND HIROYO YOKOYAMA

There was drama behind the marriage of Nihei Yokoyama and Hiroyo Yoneda centering about Nihei telling Hiroyo that he would marry her but that life with him would be difficult. Nihei was peddling shoes at farm camps across California. Nihei was not a man of any great wealth. When Nihei welcomed Emi and Hozumi, he was gardening in Monrovia.

What Nihei meant by his remark was that Hiroyo would have to work hard in helping Nihei with his travels, his shoe inventory, and later, his work as a gardener, as well as giving birth to seven children. Hiroyo was a busy housewife, mother, and worker with Nihei inasmuch as Nihei was a slightly built man who demanded attention.

Hiroyo passed away on New Year's Day, 1940.

As an aside, it is fair to note that Bill, Nihei's third son, often told me the story of how he missed seeing his mother, Hiroyo, pass away because of New Year's Eve events with his friends. She was so dear to the Yokoyama family.

The Issei and Kibei of that era suffered not only economically, but also, socially . . . every kid wanting his day in the sun.

The Issei were first generation Japanese, whereas Kibei were those born in America, went to Japan, and returned to America.

*Emi, Karl, and Hozumi, pictured here, are Kibei.*

Emi, older brother Goso or better known later as Karl, and Hozumi were all Kibei Nisei (second generation inasmuch as they were born in California).

Guys, like Emi's brother, Karl, could not afford shoes, and so, he made *geta* (wooden clogs) and walked around in them.

Nihei's older children, George, Harry, and Bill, worked hard to help the slight Nihei get his gardening jobs completed.

Nihei, with his seven kids, needed to have Emi and Hozumi find jobs inasmuch as he could not support them for a period of time. Therefore, Emi got sent to the Okumura market in Boyle Heights while Hozumi went to another household to work.

Nihei brokered a deal where Emi and Hozumi were to be wed to Morizo Fujimoto and Isamu Kawamoto. However it was done, by the end of the day, Nihei sent Emi to Morizo in 1927.

I heard one story where Emi was shown photographs of Morizo and Isamu. Since Emi was the *neesan* (older sister), she got to select first and chose Morizo. Thus, Nihei shed his burden and his obligation, his *On* (honor).

Pictured are Morizo and Emi Annie for their wedding at the Buddhist Temple of San Diego (BTSD).

I was born in 1928. My journey through life started with their marriage.

# MORIZO IN SUNNYSIDE (1927-1937)

Jolene, my daughter, wrote an interview with Emi for a UCLA Asian American Studies class in which she was told that Morizo and Emi spent their first days living in a barn, not a house. Emi was disappointed. Furthermore, not having any knowledge of farming, except the few times that she cultivated silkworms, she was aghast that Morizo and she would seek leased land funded by Emi's brother, Karl. Morizo was poor and had very few assets.

Morizo and Emi stayed in Sunnyside, a small town in the suburbs of San Diego outside the town of Chula Vista. The town was a market and gasoline stand located between Bonita and Sweetwater Dam.

It was ten years before they would move to Encinitas in Northern San Diego County in 1937.

Here, I want to chronicle some events that I recall about Morizo as a father, teacher, counselor, along with being a transmitter of values that I still cherish to this day.

Jack Fujimoto

## MORIZO AND THE FARM

Morizo leased twenty acres of level farmland from Burris, owner of the adjacent dairy. There was a creek running through the central portion of the farm. A small house with shed and outhouse was leased along with the farmland. Morizo, as was his custom throughout his life, probably built the bathhouse (*ofuro*) away from the house.

The ancillary facilities of shed, outhouse, and bathhouse were significant in that it influenced me tremendously, as I spent those ten years on the Sunnyside property.

Our main house was located at the base of a hill. The cows of Burris's dairy ate the grass growing on the hillside. The hillside provided much enjoyment for Fumi, Yo, and me inasmuch as we would take a sheet of tin used on the side of barns and took them up that hill to slide down, most of the time quite smoothly.

Burris appeared to have extensive holdings of land of which Morizo leased a small portion.

*Pictured are Emi and Morizo in their work clothes. Typically, the mornings in Sunnyside were cool, so they had to bundle up and shed the coats and jackets during the day of work.*

Neither Morizo nor Emi had any training for growing vegetables and so, coming shortly to a married life along with farming was quite an experience as well as challenge. Morizo spent time on farms to know what to grow and harvest, but not much knowledge on the intricacies of farming operations.

Emi had no background in farming, let alone only feeding silkworms back in her hometown of Yasuno Village in Hiroshima. As Jolene stated in her paper, Emi had doubts about surviving if Morizo pursued his Frank Wiggins diesel mechanics training.

The learning curve for farming must have been challenging.

Preparing the soil for planting seeds or nursery stock, providing water and nutrients, growth with pesticides (if needed), and harvesting probably were primary areas of concern in their first year on the Sunnyside property.

There was the issue of my being born in 1928, which made it difficult for Emi to do much work on the farm.

Fumi and Yo in those early years helped much in the area of crop irrigation. Their work is described here with the use of flumes.

Crops were grown in a north-south direction with water being directed by flumes that were stacked to guide water flow. Flumes were usually six by six-inch pieces of lumber nailed together six or eight feet in length. Holes were drilled in each flume spaced apart to have water flow down each furrow. When water reached the end of each row, the hole was plugged with paper and an additional hole was opened or another flume added. Fumi and Yo may have been available to plug the holes, but I doubt that they could add additional flumes or even carry one.

The flumes were moved from place to place by Morizo as they were quite heavy and Morizo did not have any employed labor . . . just Emi, my mother, and me.

So, Morizo planted crops that did not need extensive water. I remember the onions and garlic especially, and some bean crops such as dry lima beans were planted because of concern for water usage and did not require flumes for irrigation.

On the north side of the farm, a two-lane road went east-west lined with rows of pepper trees that occasionally attracted a crowd when peppercorns were ripe. It was an asphalted road, and therefore, did not kick up a lot of dust.

On the west side of the farm was a major artery leading to the Burris dairy going south. Its northern terminus was the village of Sunnyside, made up of a gas station, a small grocery store, and bus stop for us going to school. The creek on our farm had its water go under the road through large concrete cisterns buried under the road. So, the water from the creek flowed quite well on the farm.

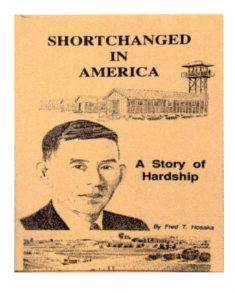

*Pictured is the book about the Hosaka family written by Fred T. Hosaka entitled Shortchanged in America, A Story of Hardship. Published by Fred T. Hosaka, 175 pages, on January 1, 1993, ASIN B0006F3EE1.*

Across the west side of the street was the Hosaka farm. Fred Tomio Hosaka, one of the Hosaka brothers, wrote a book about the Hosaka family and their travails.

Minetaro Hosaka moved his family from the Mission Valley area of San Diego to Sunnyside. They were established farmers before Morizo and Emi moved to Sunnyside.

I did not go over to visit much but recall that Minetaro had quite a large family. Gus, his oldest, was a fisherman out of San Diego Harbor. Fred and John were more my contemporaries but I very seldom saw them.

Kimiko was a daughter who became a Kuratomi and who I saw much later in life when she was an active Nisei in Los Angeles.

Morizo did not visit them except occasionally when social visits for a donation to a San Diego NihonJin Kai event.

## LIFE ON THE FARM

From the farm, we could see Mount Soledad, a landmark for the Sunnyside village and adjacent Sweetwater Dam and River.

When it rained, the creek got filled, but I do not recall it ever flooding. Often, to cross the creek on rainy days, Morizo had to carry Fumi and Yo across so that they could get to the bus stop and get to Chula Vista Elementary School. They said they enjoyed being carried on his back.

The loamy farm soil was quite productive. Morizo poured much chicken manure into the property by shovel . . . manual labor. Often that manual labor was me. Spreading the smelly and sticky chicken manure was a tedious job. Chicken manure did not flake uniformly like horse manure, which was much easier to toss and it would flake rather uniformly across a field. For a youngster of seven or eight, it was a good body-building exercise.

When the produce such as cucumbers, peppers, onions, and garlic were shipped and commanded high prices at the San Diego

Produce Market, I felt satisfied that I had a hand in its growth. Often, I took a break to go to the Burris dairy for liquid refreshment, the milk dripping off of the coolers.

Morizo had a one-ton stake truck, Chevrolet, I believe. He also had a tractor with disc, plow, and trailer. He had a horse, chickens around the house, and many gophers, as I recall. Emi had a cute white dog, much like a miniature shepherd.

*Pictured is Emi holding Yoko with Morizo looking along with Fumie in front and Jack behind Morizo. The venue was the Japanese Hospital (Nihon Byoin) in East Los Angeles.*

Fumie, Yoko, and I were born on the Sunnyside property. I was born in 1928, Fumie in 1931, and Yoko in 1933.

The remainder of the Morizo family of Takashi, Judy, and Eiko were born after leaving Sunnyside for Encinitas, they were sort of a second family.

## THE TEMPLE AND MORIZO

Morizo was a young member of the Buddhist Temple of San Diego (BTSD) located on Market Street in the eastern section of San Diego. The resident minister was Reverend Nishii.

About the time of the Great Depression in the US and the stock market crash with many people out of jobs and starving, Reverend Nishii formed the Young Men's Buddhist Association (YMBA) in the late 1920s. The first president of the young group was Morizo, elected in 1929. One of Morizo's strong supporters was Zembei Iwashita.

Morizo must have had considerable charisma and leadership ability to undertake this role. I recall that he was interested in *shibai,* a role-playing script acted out on some aspect from Japanese history. At the time, the temple served as a community center for Issei immigrants.

Members of the Japan Association (*NihonJin Kai*) met on 5$^{th}$ Avenue in downtown San Diego near the Kawasaki Market. But talent shows such as the *shibai* as well as community events were held at the Buddhist temple as well as the Ocean View Christian Church. Often, the *shibai* was choreographed with a historic Japanese event in which temple members participated. After all, these ways of entertainment drew members to be a stronger community.

*This was a hanamatsuri (flower festival) production. It is an annual celebration in the Buddhist community to celebrate the historical Shakamuni Buddha's birthday. Morizo is third from left in uniform.*

## MORIZO AND LANGUAGE SCHOOL

Morizo not only supported the temple and its activities, but also its Japanese language school. Japanese language classes were held on Saturdays while temple services were on Sundays. So, Morizo often had to spend the weekends driving from Sunnyside through Bonita and National City to get to the temple.

I do not recall what he did on a harvest day that usually fell on Sunday. In any event, Morizo seemed to be busy.

Morizo kept his Japanese language roots. Throughout his life, he wrote in the Japanese language. He often wrote his diary in Japanese rather than in English.

The language school used the official Japanese Ministry of Education readers. They were difficult books for readers like me who had to struggle with the English language because much of the speaking at home was done in Japanese.

## FAMILY SUPPORT IN THE 1930 DECADE

In the 1930s, I recall that many members of the temple as well as students from its affiliated Japanese language school were encouraged along with members of the community to save "tinfoil" from cigarette wrappers so that they could be combined with *imon bukuro* (special relief packages) that were sent to Japan to help Japanese families.

The 1930s were difficult years for our relatives in Japan. The military cliques dominated much activity such as Japan's expansion into Manchuria (called *Manshukoku*) (満洲国) in the early 1930s, the Sino-Japan conflict in 1937, and the Nomonhan defeat that changed the entire outlook of Japan's expansionist ambitions. Japan's scarce resources were being depleted and our relatives had scarcities showing. So, they welcomed any relief packages.

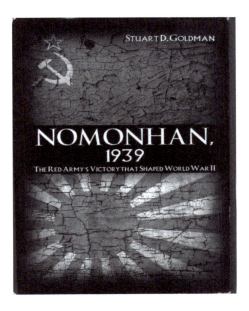

*Stuart D. Goldman, Nomonhan 1939: The Red Army's Victory That Shaped World War II, Naval Institute Press, Annapolis, MD, 2012*

Any serious student of Japanese history of the 1930s should read about the battle of Nomonhan in Mongolia where the General Tojo directed "crack" Kwangtung Japanese army was defeated by the Soviets which turned the direction of the Pacific War (World War II).

From the book, the defeat at Nomonhan in Mongolia shifted the emperor and his advisers to stop the Soviet invasion towards the oil rich Southeast Asia. Japan needed resources that could have been secured with a Japanese victory at Nomonhan and further push into the Soviet Union, but that was not to be.

## MEMBERS AND FRIENDS

I started attending the Buddhist temple in 1933, age five, to learn the Japanese language on Saturday as well as going to religious services on Sunday. Going to Sunday services was more difficult because crops were usually cut or picked on Sunday for delivery to the San Diego Produce Market. Morizo usually made deliveries to the market on Sunday, Tuesday, and Thursday.

The Japanese language classes during the 1930s had many familiar names and faces whom I chummed with at school and later, got to see in our professional lives. Ruth Takahashi Voorhees comes to mind. Among her friends were Mitsuko Adachi (whose parents originally lived in Yasuno-mura in Hiroshima near my mother's ancestral home), and Meg Hatada. These girls were a few years older but provided opportunities to learn about community events. To this day, I still have contact with Ruth.

*Pictured is Reverend Jim Yanagihara and me at the Fresno Vintage Home, Fresno, California.*

Recently, I saw Reverend Jim Yanagihara in Fresno's Vintage Home, prior to his passing. At the BTSD Japanese language school, Jim was called "Gopher." After many years, addressing Reverend Jim as Gopher was a strange feeling, but he responded, and so, I thought that nicknames during our early years can elicit a laugh. Nicknames were common among us. Reverend Jim was a popular Jodo Shinshu Buddhist minister during his professional years.

Walter Fujimoto, no relation, and Masato Asakawa were classmates at school. Kawamoto, Honda, and Himaka had several family members attending the Japanese language classes.

*Pictured are Yutaka and Hisayo flanking Reverend Nishii in the front row. In the back row are Morizo (on left) and Zembei Iwashita (on right). Middle person is unknown.*

## WANTING TO KNOW ABOUT BUDDHISM

As for Sunday school classes (Dharma school is present-day nomenclature), I did not attend enough times to get any attendance certificate; however, my interest as well as initiation into the Buddhist religion, philosophy, and rituals started at a young age. Young as I was, I asked often about death and dying. Why do we die? What happens when we die? Where do we go? On and on with questions, often asking such questions in the truck taking produce to the San Diego Produce Market.

Patiently, Morizo provided some background and information to satisfy my queries.

## EDUCATION IN NIHONGO

Morizo was also interested in academics. He helped me with my learning of the Japanese language. He enrolled me in the Japanese language school held at the BTSD. He, himself, was often writing in the Japanese language whether it be a diary or larger sheets of calligraphy.

By the time we moved from Sunnyside to Encinitas, some forty miles to the northern part of San Diego County, I was in the fourth grade in the Japanese reader. It was the same reader used by students in Japan, the official text published by the Ministry of Education in Japan. Often, I neglected to complete my weekly homework assignment and so, Tokunaga Sensei, a Buddhist minister, often gave me a *pachin* stick slap on my wrist or shoulder, scolding me for not doing my homework. In later life, I met Reverend Tokunaga when he was a priest at the San Jose Buddhist Temple.

One incident in a Japanese language school assembly that I recall well was when I was assigned to talk about the Buddha (a prepared script that I had to memorize). I was not the brightest when it came to memorizing a nonnative script and told my mother that it was difficult. She immediately told me to go to the outhouse and lock myself in it until I could memorize the talk. It did not take long for me to get out of the fly-infested smelly outhouse, telling mother that I memorized it.

On the day of the talk, I think, I was in the first grade at the Japanese language school, I went to the podium, held a picture of the Buddha facing the audience, pasted my talk on the back of it, and proceeded to give my talk. It went over well. How clever I was!

At home, Morizo and Emi spoke much *Nihongo* because of their limited English skills and comfort. I do not know how my sisters, Fumie and Yoko, communicated with our father and mother because they did not learn much Japanese.

Jack Fujimoto

## DISCIPLINE AT HOME

Morizo was a patient and understanding teacher, but when I got out of line because I did not do what he wanted, I was in the woodshed only to be bailed out by my mother.

Sometimes, I went directly to the Burris dairy farm milk cooler and guzzled the refreshing milk instead of going home to the woodshed. That was my salvation because Burris gave me free access to his milk.

On one occasion, I disobeyed my father's order when he wanted me to cut the neck of a chicken in the yard so that he could have Emi serve chicken to guests. I disliked the taking of animal life. I forced myself to cut the neck of the chicken and see it dance around headless. Then, I plunged the chicken into hot water to pluck its feathers. Then, I cut it in different sections to give to my mother.

My mother was not much of a creative cook. After all, she had to look after the needs of toddlers, Fumie and Yoko, and at the same time, working with Morizo in the fields where cabbage, onions, cucumbers, and peppers were grown and trucked to market. Irrigation through ditches and flumes also had to be watched. But, on the home front, the table was typically *gohan* (rice), *tsukemono* (pickled vegetables), *umeboshi* (pickled plums), tomato soup, and occasionally, some meat.

Fumi said that our mother worked in the field to help Morizo such that she often came home late. So, she trained Fumi to cook tomato soup and rice for every night with tomatoes from the farm. In those days, we didn't have a rice cooker as we know them today. We had to watch the rice boil with enough water. On the one hand, each batch had to have enough water so that it did not coat the pan with burnt crust or water scarcity would present uncooked rice. Fumi had a responsibility just making rice for the meals each day.

For the tomato soup, it was scraps of bacon, along with salt, sugar, and water along with the chopped tomatoes.

Living next to the Burris dairy and our friendship being developed through leasing land from them, we always had ample milk to drink.

There were other incidents on the Sunnyside farm that upset Morizo, such as driving the small stake truck to capture and haul cabbage and onions. I think that I was about six years of age when I sat in the one-ton stake truck to steer it down a row of onions that were being tossed into the truck for eventual delivery to the San Diego Produce market. I veered off the row which raised the ire of Morizo. Scolding!

On another occasion, I recall driving the tractor into the edge of the creek that bisected the farm. Getting it back on to firm ground was an ordeal.

Even at a young age, I was often told to spread the truckload of chicken manure on the field for disking and plowing for the next crop. It was a job that I did not like but the alternative was the "shed."

I often took "breaks" and went to the Burris dairy to drink some unpasteurized milk flowing down the cold louvres into large vats for pasteurization and trucking to market. I can still taste it!

Milk was always available at home. I took a container with me each day to get our daily milk. So, I was often told that my growth was conditioned by drinking milk daily. After all, I weighed more than 100 pounds in the fourth grade. But, I also had caught pneumonia at one time, had a heart murmur, and generally speaking, *milk butori* (putting on weight through consumption of milk).

Although Morizo's discipline required much personal sacrifice, what he instilled in me was the appreciation of hard work, building physical strength and stamina, and gratitude to family.

When Fumi and Yo misbehaved, Morizo locked them out of the house at night. Fumi recalled crying and banging on the door for reentry. It was scary.

Generally speaking, Morizo and Emi embraced traditional Japanese values such as perseverance, patience, respect, compassion, commitment, and feel for humanity. Morizo never complained about his lot in life, his family, or in conversations. He was quite independent but not a loner. He struggled hard to eke out a living but always protected his family . . . at least, that was my lasting impression of Morizo as a man.

## TAKE NO DEBT

One personal value that Morizo cherished was to assume no debt if it could be avoided. Farming was a gamble any way you looked at it because the elements governed so much of the outcome of crops; however, to continue any extensive farm operations without hiring labor required initial capital to start, such as having basic tools and seeds. For this, produce markets often extended capital and recouped their loans through commissions earned on produce brought to market. Thrift, patience, and discipline were essential qualities exemplified by Morizo in his farming operations.

## LEARNING PERSONAL VALUES

The Sunnyside farm provided several opportunities to learn some of the traditional values that Morizo and Emi learned during their younger days.

*Enryo* (遠慮) was a traditional value inculcated into us. It meant that we should refrain from taking more than we should or be humble and reserved.

*Gaman* (我慢) was another value that we observed. Whereas others might have better pleasures of life, if we could not afford it, we refrain from asking and use what we had. Morizo's "take no debt" is a good example that we practiced.

*Gimu* ( 義務 ) is to follow through on obligations that we incur. When we say or promise, we should complete the task.

*Ninjo* ( 人情 ) is to be kind and gentle to others with humility and humanity . . . lots of compassion.

These are some of the commonsense personal values that our parents instilled in us as we lived on the Sunnyside farm.

## SOCIAL EVENTS

Since we lived in the rural section outside of Chula Vista, our social contacts were limited to visits to our neighbor, the Burris dairy owners, as well as the other neighbor, the Hosaka family: Minetaro, the father; and his children, Gus, Fred, John, and Kimiko. They lived across the street. To this day, I have wondered why, as neighbors, Morizo did not socialize more with the Hosaka family. Even in Fred's book on his father's struggle in farming, Morizo is a nonentity, no mention at all. Morizo went to the same Buddhist Temple of San Diego as Fred's father.

During the week when Morizo took his produce to market, he often stopped by Yutaka's ranch in Logan Heights to pick up his produce and take it to market along with his produce. Then, after delivery, his routine included visiting the Japanese Association meetings on 5th Avenue. He gave me a quarter to see a Western movie while he attended his meeting. I got to know Butch Cassidy, Roy Rogers, Tom Mix, and other Western movie stars.

Or, Morizo went to the Buddhist Temple of San Diego to have meetings in which his friend, Zembei Iwashita, was involved. They often conspired on the next *shibai* (usually a drama based on some historical event).

During summer months, Morizo helped with the Hiroshima Kenjin Kai picnics at one of the beaches in the South Bay. There, the kids enjoyed not only the eats, but also the many goodies, usually school supplies such as notebooks, pencils, rulers, and stationery passed out for participating in various events: running events, donut eating, rope pull, and others.

When we did not participate in community-wide social events or contacts with others, Morizo encouraged us to have fun at home.

We learned *hana fuda*, a Japanese card game. Morizo liked to play solitaire and blackjack "21" cards where he used nuts instead of money.

On rainy days, we stayed in the house watching our white-haired dog that my mother loved. After the rain, Fumi, Yo, and I took a sheet of stainless-steel metal to the top of the hill behind the house and rode it downhill in the mud. Dirty, muddy, and heaped with grass, it did not matter, we were having fun.

## INTERACTING WITH COUSINS

During the summer, I often stayed with my cousins in Logan Heights of San Diego. They had a large mulberry tree with ripe fruit. Gorging myself with mulberries was terrific.

Summer often meant the harvesting of tomatoes. After the main crop of tomatoes were harvested and sent to market, Akiko and Archie, my cousins, and I went around the bush tomato vines to pick the "culls," which we boxed and sold at a makeshift produce stand on a busy thoroughfare in Logan Heights. Even selling the produce at a quarter a box resulted in considerable spending change for the three of us. We did this for several summers. So, I looked forward to visiting and staying with Yutaka's kids.

I also learned much from Archie during these stays. He was always doing something with electronics, making a Heathkit radio, a ham radio station, or some other device ordered through advertisements in *Popular Mechanics*, *Popular Science*, or the local paper. Archie was quite curious and creative.

## GOING TO SCHOOL

I walked from home to the school bus station, some miles away, to catch the bus to go to Chula Vista Elementary School through the beginning of my fifth grade.

I learned a valuable lesson at the small market run by an old man. I liked a caramel candy called Walnettos at that time. I took one which the old man saw me take. He scolded me saying that if you want anything, always ask for it. You will hear immediately, "yes" or "no." This admonition has stayed with me through my life, thanks to that old man, "Pops."

I do not recall Morizo ever coming to the school except for a drop-off; however, my mother, Emi, had to go on several occasions to have the school nurse talk to her about me . . . too heavy for my age (110 pounds, too fat), heart murmur, lung issues. On some occasions, I went to school without shoes because I was flat-footed and could not find shoes comfortable or wide enough to wear. I never heard a complaint from Morizo about these visits.

At times, though, Morizo asked about my being late to come home from school. I could not tell him that I had taken a friend, Dorothy Winkler, home. I rode the bus to her stop and walked home after she got off. I found a good companion in her who also liked to raid the fruit trees near our houses . . . we usually knew the tree owners.

Jack Fujimoto

## OTHER EXPERIENCES
## FISHING

Morizo sometimes took me with him to nearby Sweetwater Dam and its downstream tributary. We had makeshift poles, line with sinker, and some bait, often a ball of bread, or earthworms. We looked for perch or bass, often perch being easier to catch. Tasted good when deep-fried.

This was a seldom experience because Morizo was busy with his farm.

## VISITS BY KARL YONEDA, EMI'S BROTHER

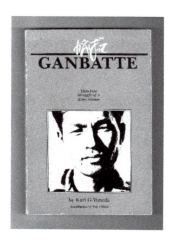

*Karl G. Yoneda, Ganbatte: Sixty Year Struggle of a Kibei Worker, 1983, Resource Development and Publications, Asian American Studies Center, University of California, Los Angeles*

Sometimes, Karl Goso Yoneda came to recuperate from his many encounters with the Los Angeles Police. He was involved with organizing labor groups. He was especially well-known as an effective activist for Japanese working laborers in Los Angeles. At one time, he was editor of the *Rodo Shimbun* (Labor News). These incidents are well documented in his book, *Ganbatte*, that chronicles his struggles to organize Japanese laborers.

## VISIT BY RELATIVES

On other occasions, Nihei Yokoyama and his family or Emi's cousins, Hitoshi and Narumi Yoneda, came to visit. It is on those occasions that I often had to slaughter a chicken so that it could be served to our guests.

I do not recall too many guests coming over to spend time with Morizo and Emi. It was more that Morizo visited others while Emi stayed home with Fumie and Yoko. I recall Emi doing crocheting and knitting.

## LIFE ON THE HOME FRONT

As mentioned before, Emi often worked side by side with Morizo in the field. As Fumie recalled, they came home late. Emi taught Fumie to cook in order to conserve Emi's time.

Fumie told the story of taking sandwiches to elementary school in Chula Vista. The sandwiches were made early in the morning with mayonnaise and sliced tomato on Wonder Bread. By lunchtime, the sandwiches were so soggy that it was most difficult to eat.

Morizo, at times, cooked. His turtle soup was delicious, but where he got his turtle was a mystery and still cannot be recalled. Occasionally, he made pancakes on the potbellied stove in the living room. Morizo rose to the occasion when we needed food and Emi was unavailable.

*In this older picture, Morizo is holding a kampai (BOTTOMS UP) cup and with one swig, empties the cup. In his Sunnyside days, Morizo did not show any liking for alcohol and I did not observe his drinking alcoholic beverages. In later life, he was a one-sipper before his getting red and flushed. That was a good lesson for me.*

# MORIZO IN ENCINITAS (1937-1942)

## GETTING SETTLED IN ENCINITAS

Morizo moved his family from Sunnyside, south of San Diego, in April 1937, to Encinitas, north of San Diego, some fifty miles apart. The move was primarily prompted by Morizo's brother, Yutaka, moving from Logan Heights in San Diego, to take over a strawberry farm in the northern section of Encinitas. Strawberries are a labor-intensive crop. The farm was probably thirty-plus acres because there were four labor camps attached to it.

The Oye Family who had been growing strawberries there decided to pull up roots and return to Japan.

## MOVING FROM SUNNYSIDE TO ENCINITAS

Moving from Sunnyside was not an easy task. There was a limited three acres of land adjacent to the Yutaka farm. So, if Morizo wanted to farm more extensively, he had to remove bushes, trees, and cacti from a side of a hill to open new farmland. That would produce another twenty acres of leased land that he could use to grow vegetables for the Los Angeles Produce Market. Opening a shipping operation would be difficult for produce from the two brothers' farms, because scale of operation would be difficult without adequate capital. The Los Angeles market was at least 100 miles away, whereas the San Diego market was about forty miles away. Besides, Yutaka was more into berries, whereas Morizo was focused on vegetables. A shipping operation was out of the question.

## ITARU AND HAYATO OKABEPPU FROM JAPAN

Yutaka summoned Itaru and Hayato Okabeppu from Kagoshima, Japan, in 1935 to come to Encinitas to help with farming operations. After all, the Okabeppu family had returned to Japan, with Itaru and Hayato staying at the Yasukichi Fujimoto homestead, and attending Shiwa Elementary School, the school that Morizo attended during his early years.

Itaru was more of an artist, preferring the sedentary life on an established farm such as Yutaka's. Hayato was an outdoors type of guy interested in mechanics and repairing equipment.

*Pictured from left to right: Jack, Itaru, Sumiko, Yutaka, Yukie, Hisayo, Morizo, Yoko, Akiyoshi, Emi, Hayato, Fumie, Akiko.*

Yutaka and Hisayo had Akiko, Akiyoshi, Sumiko, and Yukie as part of their family. Seiko would come later to make their family.

The Morizo and Emi family had Jack, Fumie, and Yoko. Later, Takashi, Fujie, and Eiko would join the family.

Hayato and Itaru had just come from Kagoshima, Japan, to work on the farms.

## DEVELOPING ACREAGE

In 1937, when Morizo went to Encinitas to farm near Yutaka, Hayato was available to help.

With California's Alien Land Law in effect, it was possible to buy undeveloped land in my name as a child of nine years old, but Morizo opted to lease some undeveloped land near Yutaka's ranch. He leased some twenty acres from the San Dieguito Irrigation District and Helen Stuart, the undeveloped land located east of Burgundy Road and north of Capri Road.

I, along with my cousin, Archie (short for Akiyoshi), often worked alongside Morizo and Hayato to level the land for planting of crops, beans, eggplant, various squashes and peppers, some berries other than strawberries, tomatoes, and cucumbers.

Archie, at age eleven, and me at age nine, could not contribute much to the pulling of stumps of bushes, small trees, cactus, yucca plants, and myriad of plants interspersed among rocks, but outside of school, I recall enjoying what we did. Making the land arable brought further problems. Wild animals, rodents, and poisonous animals posed their own problem.

Irrigating with furrows with flumes like in Sunnyside? Or go to some other method that required less intense labor? Yutaka had large deep furrows for his berries. Eventually, Morizo used a modified sprinkler system of irrigation on most of his acreage.

In the second year of growing beans on the developed property, I recall that Archie was helping in the harvest of Kentucky Wonder beans and got stung by a scorpion in his crotch.

Panic!

Rushed to a clinic, he recovered. That was quite a lesson learned.

The developed landscape had snakes as well as centipedes. But there were also lots of gophers, squirrels, and rabbits. Shooting rabbits for a meal was an isolated incident but for us, often it was the only meat readily available.

## VISITING NEIGHBOR, SEYMOUR

I often had to water the crops. It was a time-consuming job but did leave time to visit "old man" Seymour, a bachelor, living near the southern edge of Morizo's farm on the west side of Burgundy Road. Seymour reminded me of the popular Popeye cartoon character with his crooked mouth and jutting jaw.

Seymour cultivated many fruit trees, some of which were unknown to me at first: sapota, cherimoya, guava. Others were citrus and deciduous. So, I got to know Seymour quite well, and so, often it was "Come on over, Jack," and we enjoyed some fruit in season. I liked the exotic fruit, especially the sapota.

## VISIT TO LOIBL

Sometimes, I went to the Loibl house, a gated palace-like structure, adjacent to Seymour's property. I very seldom saw "old man Loibl." I do not know that Morizo ever spoke to him. Loibl had substantial acreage featuring many citrus trees, naval and Valencia oranges, along with grapefruit, tangerines, tangelos, and kumquats. I was less eager to eat those fruits as compared to what Seymour had.

## HOUSING

Whereas Yutaka bought the ongoing strawberry operation from Oye that included farm labor dwellings, Morizo had to build his family home. When Morizo moved his family to Encinitas, our family occupied one of Yutaka's labor camps.

Morizo and Hayato built a modest wooden structure that became our home. What appeared was a smaller wood-framed house, a shed to house equipment and tools, along with an outhouse, a separate building for bathing, and cages for pigeons, and shelter for chickens. Adjacent to the house, Morizo and Hayato built a produce-packing house along with loading dock. Hayato was an ideal young man to help in constructing all of these structures.

## OUTHOUSE

The outhouse was a "hole in the ground" in back of the house. It was usually a "one holer," rather than a "two holer." When it filled up, we just moved the structure over another hole. It was often my task to dig the holes. In some spots, I recall, the soil below a couple of feet was "hardpan" and therefore, difficult to penetrate . . . so, move on and find a softer spot.

For hospitality in the outhouse, we used any newsprint. Morizo used the newspapers for his bathhouse kindling wood whenever available and so, the catalogs of Montgomery Ward, Sears, Roebuck, and Spiegels were especially welcomed. I guess if worse came to worse, we could have used the abundant cactus to wipe ourselves after cutting off the prickly thorns.

Later in life, when someone asked me about my future career, I often laughed and said that I might become a "shit engineer." I surely had credentials for digging "outhouses."

## BATHHOUSE

Morizo always liked his bathhouse. He did not care much for the indoor tub or bathtub being in the house. He always liked a separate structure where he placed a stainless-steel bathtub on top of wrought iron bedded on concrete blocks. A wooden palette was installed in the tub so that our body would not be scalded by the touch of metal to body.

Just about every night, Morizo took delight in taking some newsprint and twigs or branches from the hillside near the house, light the fire, and watch as it heated the bathtub of water. He loved the fire. In cold weather, he would hover over the fire warming himself.

When the water in the tub was hot, the traditional pecking order took place with the oldest male and all males taking a bath followed by the females.

On entering the bathhouse with *geta* (wooden clogs), disrobing, pouring some hot water over the body, and getting into the hot water slowly, and resting for a while to sense the body soothed by the hot water, get out, suds up, vigorously cleanse the body, and wash off before getting into the hot water again. That was the usual routine.

Sometimes, Morizo would be outside the bathhouse without any bathrobe or clothes, naked to the elements, and apparently feeling good! Such behavior would be difficult in the urban centers.

Some have commented that a good healthy body can be promoted by the Nishiki method of bathing, that is, take a hot-water dip followed by a cold-water dip, do for one, two, or even three times each time. I tried it in Honolulu when we stopped over visiting Mr. Higa of Daikoku Tei and his catering business.

Higa-san had his bathtub separate from the main house. His Nishiki method of bathing I adopted and used when visiting *Onsen* in Japan.

I never discussed this aspect of Nishiki bathing with Morizo.

## THE JUNKYARD

Between Yutaka's labor camps and where Morizo built our house, was a junkyard. Over the years, much unwanted equipment, structures, gadgets, and devices were abandoned. In some cases, Morizo and Hayato could find useful vessels such as commodes for feeding pigeons and chickens. Or, they found leftover auto parts for growing flowers and left them to adorn the newly built house. Amazing what can be made from unwanted stuff!

On one occasion, Hayato and Archie used a trailer in the junkyard to build their rowboat that was to be used in the slough adjacent to the ranch. After designing the craft, gluing together essential parts, and assembling it over time, they took it to the slough where it survived. But, when they took it out to sea, with the first wave, it became unglued and returned in splinters. But, in hindsight, it was fun.

The junkyard served as a buffer between Yutaka's labor camp and our home. Since it was open space, the plow, harrowing equipment, disk, and other farm equipment were stored. Some irrigating equipment was often housed there. Sprinklers were a common commodity there.

## MAIN HOUSE — WOODEN STRUCTURE

The main house faced the Pacific Ocean. It was built on a knoll that had a good view of the ocean. Later, when World War II broke out on December 7, 1941, this view caused considerable inquiry from the FBI.

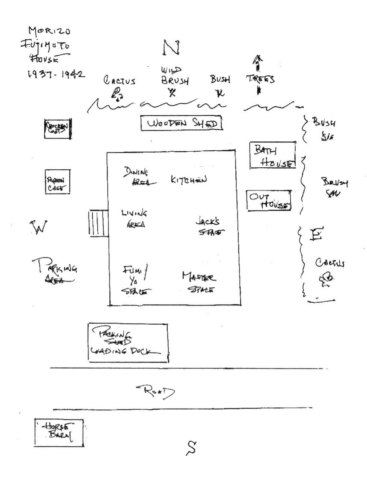

The back side faced a fifteen-degree slope looking towards a high hill with much cactus and bushes along the view. The back side of the house led to the outhouse and bathhouse along with a wooden shed.

The front side of the house had the pigeon cage and chicken coop. Climbing the stairs to the front entry to the house, one encountered the living room that led to a dining area and kitchen to the left and the master bedroom and bedroom for Fumi and Yo. My room was directly east of the living room. This was a modest wooden structure.

To the south of the house was the main road fronting the packing shed, equipment storage barn, and just west on the road was the horse corral.

## THE FARM

Morizo had one hired hand, a Mexican named Reynoso. Otherwise, the labor was Morizo, Hayato, sometimes my mother, Emi, and when not in school, me, Fumi, and Yo.

Hayato's younger brothers, Akira and Takeshi, came in 1937, but basically worked on the Yutaka ranch.

During the working week, the packing shed was where our family gathered after early morning harvest.

My mother, Emi, did much of the tomato packing since it brought better prices when it was a five by six or six by six. Larger or smaller such as three by five or seven by eight did not sell well at the terminal or city markets in Los Angeles. My job primarily was to nail covers over the premium fruit.

Bell peppers and Anaheim chili peppers were put into wired crates that I tagged and sealed. Cucumbers were sized and placed into boxes which I covered.

The John Kolbeck three-ton truck usually came late in the evening, usually 8 or 9 p.m. So, there had to be considerable lamps shining on the produce transferred.

## THE FBI SEARCH

When December 7, 1941, found the United States announcing war with Japan, those lamps and, in fact, our many lights caused several FBI visits. Questions such as "communicating with Jap sub out there?" were frequently asked.

With wartime hysteria heightened with news of an enemy submarine seen off the Santa Barbara coastline, it was inevitable that we would be a prime target. From our home and shed, the Pacific Ocean was clear and easy to see.

Between December 1941 and May 1942, we were visited on numerous occasions by the FBI. I took whatever radio communications equipment we had to leave among the cacti. The FBI queried me, not Morizo because of his limited English. I was thirteen at the time.

All cameras, Japanese language books, newsprint, and whatever else that might be considered contraband was taken up the hill to the east of the house and hidden. Photograph albums and the like were too numerous for me to carry up the hill. We did not have any controversial equipment, but were a prime target for FBI search, much more than Yutaka's house because we were so visible to the Pacific Ocean.

## THE COMMUNITY CENTER

The Encinitas–Leucadia–Solana Beach–Del Mar area had a handful of Japanese American or Nikkei families. The few families often gathered monthly to discuss matters of concern. I recall visiting the Tateishi family in Del Mar where the kids played capture the flag and other games in the dark while family matters were discussed among the adults.

The Furuya family in Solana Beach had no kids and so, the kids did not visit.

The Nakagawa, Funaki, and Nakamura families were related with most of their children older than us, and therefore, contact was limited.

From the various meetings was borne the idea that a community center would be welcome to the Nikkei families. Particulars are unknown except that Morizo was one of the Japanese language teachers for the limited number of students.

In May 1942, when the US government through its $6^{th}$ Army directive forced us to go to the Poston relocation camp, we boarded our belongings at this small community center.

Personally, I do not remember much about the community center on Balford Road between Rancho Santa Fe Drive and Encinitas Road.

## REMEMBRANCES OF SOCIAL EVENTS TO THE LOS ANGELES PRODUCE MARKET

Annually, Morizo wanted to go to the Los Angeles produce markets to check commission merchants on their "take" for fees. Some years, Morizo shipped to H&F Market and Venice Celery Growers in the city market because the "net" was better than in the terminal market on Central Avenue. Hayato was usually the driver. I liked to tag along because the visit usually ended with dinner at the San Kwo Low Chinese restaurant on East First Street in Little Tokyo. That was a treat.

## FISHING

Sometimes, Hayato drove us to Box Canyon in Olivenhain where the down flow of Lake Hodges water had perch, bass, and crappy in it. If fortunate, we would catch a "fill" without any game warden search, take it home, and Mom would fry it to a crisp. This was a great source of protein for us.

Fishing on Lake Hodges from rowboats was less productive.

## WINE AND GRAPES

Yutaka liked his wine and grape juice. Hayato drove to Escondido during grape harvest season to buy lugs of different grapes. They were brought to the back of Yutaka's house to put into barrels. Archie and I were designated "grape stompers," and so we stomped on the grapes in each barrel. Our feet usually were deep purple when we got out of the barrel.

The fresh grape juice was delicious. The wine was Yutaka's interest. How and what he did or even how he made his wine, I do not recall.

*The photograph shows the fifth-grade class with me easily identified. I was the Japanese kid in the back row on the left side.*

## GOING TO SCHOOL

I started Encinitas Elementary School in the fifth grade (April 1937), the only Asian or Japanese American in class. I stood out in racial pigmentation, different from the "white" kids, but do not recall being treated differently.

We had a long walk from home to the bus stop. Usually, Fumi, Yo, and I stopped at Yutaka's house and walked with Akiko, Akiyoshi, Sumiko, and Yukie down the canyon and up a trail to the bus stop. The bus stop was a gladiola seed bed company where guys took old gladiola flower bulbs, shucked them, and repackaged them for resale.

Rainy days were a problem because the trail got awfully slippery.

Sometimes, when we stopped at the Yutaka house, we asked whether we could have one of their lunch-bag sandwiches. Our mom never put bologna or other meat into a sandwich, whereas Hisayo Obasan or Akiko, living in a labor camp and serving laborers had meat. Many times, I longed for a sandwich of Wonder Bread with a dab of butter or mayo with bologna in between.

During those Encinitas years, I went from Encinitas Elementary to San Dieguito where the junior and senior high schools were in a single location. It was much further and so, if I missed a bus ride, a five-mile hike is what confronted me.

At San Dieguito, classmates included Kaz Kosaka and Joyce Nakamura.

## EDUCATION IN JAPAN

In 1940 and 1941, there was serious talk between Morizo and Yutaka about sending Akiyoshi and me to Shiwa to live with Grandfather Yasukichi and go to school there. After all, they were making deposits at the Yokohama Specie Bank, a Japanese bank. However, in early 1940, I heard that they abandoned the plan to wait another year for reconsideration. So, in 1941, serious talk opened again. This time, family conditions changed, other matters had to be considered and no longer did Morizo want to send me to Shiwa. But, I figured that Morizo wanted to give me a better opportunity for a career with a Japanese education rather than staying in America.

In those Encinitas years, Takashi and Judy were born, and that made five children to raise. Mom's work increased considerably.

My going to Shiwa would become more of a worry. Japan was at war with China. If I were conscripted to serve in Japan's military, that would become more of a worrisome burden. How would Yasukichi, an old man, have me living with him? I am sure that Morizo put a lot of thought into his decision to have me stay with the family in Encinitas.

## SOCIAL EVENTS

*This is a rare photograph where Japanese ladies assembled to have some type of social event at the Encinitas beach. At the left side is Emi, my mother, and next to her is my aunt, Hisayo, Yutaka's wife.*

# MORIZO AND POSTON CAMP

## PREPARING TO LEAVE HOME, MAY 19, 1942
## THE PACIFIC WAR

In 1941, the Pacific War started with America and Japan as enemies. Being from Japanese ancestry living in Encinitas, California, and going to San Dieguito High School, walking some distance to the bus stop and catching the bus to school, some trying moments were had.

I was in the eighth grade. There were a few Japanese American or Nikkei kids at San Dieguito. Besides my cousins, Akiko, Archie, Sumiko, and Yukie Fujimoto, there were my siblings, Fumie and Yoko. Also, the Nakamura family of Eugene, Joyce, and Irene were students. Kaz Kosaka was in the eighth grade too.

The Nakagawa and Kuroye families lived in Encinitas, but not having mingled much with them, I do not recall much about them.

There was a small Nikkei population in Encinitas.

Besides the "whites," San Dieguito, as a unified school district that combined junior and senior high schools, had many Latino students from Eden Gardens. Many good looking "chicks" is what I recall.

Besides the English and Japanese languages, I picked up my dose of Spanish, especially slang terms . . . I could keep up with my Latino classmates.

With the war in full swing, there were many awkward moments of socializing at school.

The bigger problem for Morizo and Emi as a family was what do with accumulated equipment, large and small. Do they assign each of the kids what they take in evacuating our premises? Only two items could be taken is what I heard. Emi already had infant Judy to keep in mind. Do I take my baseball bat and glove? The directions from the authorities were that we had two weeks to make our decisions.

This problem of what and how much was depicted in a movie that my brother, Tak Fujimoto, a well-known American cinematographer, captured on film in *Swing Shift* but was edited out. I think that it would educate many about the severity of wartime hysteria and the life of Japanese and their children.

## EVACUATION

On May 19, 1942, surrounded by military police, we boarded the train at Oceanside Rail Depot with luggage in hand, no contraband, some clothes and blankets. My mother, Emi, had her hands full with infant Judy. Tak was three years old. So, it was up to Morizo, me, Fumi, and Yo to carry what we thought we needed. The remainder was to be stored at the Encinitas Nikkei community center unless we wanted to dispose of it. Since events happened so quickly, I do not recall that we thought too much about what to take and what not to take. Our neighbors were not nearby or close enough to ask them to look over our assets and so, whatever was left, Reynoso, the hired hand, safeguarded.

The Yutaka family and Okabeppu brothers of Hayato, Akira, and Takeshi also departed. Itaru had left his brothers in 1941 for work in the Central Valley of California and therefore, he was no longer around to be evacuated like the rest of them.

The train windows were shuttered and closed so that it was difficult to sense where the train was going. We got our meal: a sandwich and drink. This was wartime and rations were scarce.

For me, it was a different experience. I was not white, Black, or Latino. I never saw so many Japanese in such a large crowd, most of whom I never met or saw. This was the opportunity of a lifetime to see and meet many other Japanese from the Oceanside area.

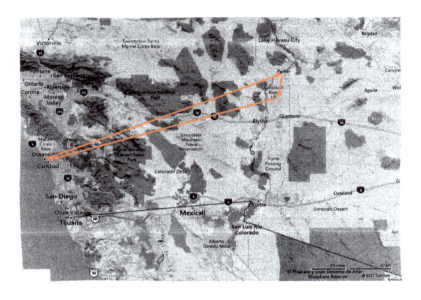

*Map shows our journey from Encinitas to Oceanside in Northern San Diego County to Parker Station, Arizona. Also shown is the journey leaving Poston Camp after WW II ends, camps are closed, and Morizo returns to Encinitas, California.*

Jack Fujimoto

## ON TO POSTON, ARIZONA, VIA PARKER STATION

We arrived in Parker, Arizona, on the outskirts of the Colorado River. This was CRIT (Colorado River Indian Tribe) country where the camp was being built. The bus took us to the newly semi-completed Poston I Camp. We were being assigned Block 28, Barrack 2, Unit D, 28-2-D.

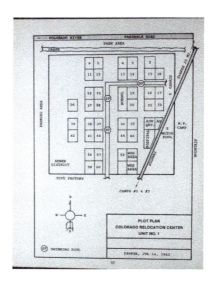

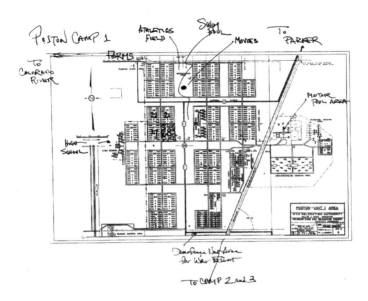

Block 28 was centrally located in Poston Camp 1. It was in a quadrant with Blocks 21, 22, and 27 as noted in the camp layout.

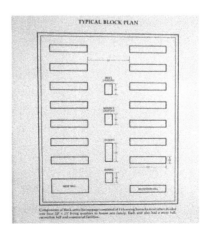

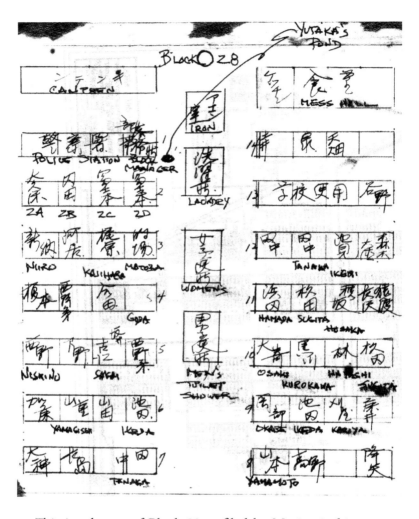

This is a layout of Block 28 as filed by Morizo in his papers. Names of residents are shown in Japanese *kanji*. The layout shows the common facilities used by block inmates, ironing room, laundry, and restrooms for women and men. No privacy.

Barrack 1: Camp police station and block manager's office.

Barrack 2: Okubo, Uchida (after my cousins, Okabeppu moved out to go to Tule Lake camp), Yutaka Fujimoto, Morizo Fujimoto.
Barrack 3: Niiro, Kawai, Kajihara, Matoba.
Barrack 4: The Goda brothers lived here, can't recall others.
Barrack 5: The Nishino families plus Sakai brothers. Isao Sakai was a classmate
Barrack 6: Kiyoshi Yamagishi and "Coyote" Ikeda lived here. Both were classmates.
Barrack 7: "Namazu" (Catfish) Kaz Tanaka was another classmate. The block library was housed in this barrack for a short period of time.
On the other side of the block was Barrack 8 housing the Yamamoto family, a large family, with father being an expert carpenter.
Barrack 9: Okabe, Ikeda (Kinjo, a martial arts teacher), Kariya (sumo teacher and camp-wide sumo participants, my sumo teachers), and Fujii.
Barrack 10: Osaki (later big-time entrepreneur in Los Angeles with beef jerky, tofu, Nanka zuke), Kurokawa, Hayashi, Sugita. Kaz Osaki was one of my teammates in camp basketball league.
Barrack 11: Henry Hamada and Art Sugita were classmates. Yuso Hamada showed me the game of "go" and "shogi." Also in this barrack was Fred and John Hosaka, the same Hosaka family that had farmed across the street from Morizo in Sunnyside in the 1930s.
Barrack 12: Tanaka, Ikemi, and Moriki. Shiz Tanaka often came over to talk to my mother, Emi. Taizo Ikemi was an avid fisherman.
Block 13: Mainly used for storage of school supplies.
Block 14: Doi, Izumi.

The two large buildings were the block mess hall and the camp canteen for purchases of supplies.

# GETTING SETTLED IN CAMP

The barrack was yet to be finished. Inside our segment of the barrack, lots of open spaces. It was a "rush" job. Tar paper did not cover much of the cracks between boards as evidenced by the wind blowing into the barrack. We needed to get cots and straw mattresses for bedding. We did not need many blankets because it was late spring and the weather was heating up.

I went to the woodpile to get some scrap wood and borrow craftsman tools to make a room barrier to separate sleeping quarters from a living area. Morizo and Emi, along with five kids, found us cramped for space in a twenty-by-twenty room. Also, I was able to make chairs or sitting stools along with tables from leftover wood.

## EMI OVERCOMES HIGH FEVER TO SURVIVE

*Pictured is my mother, Emi.*

The summer heat was overwhelming to us who came from the ocean side of California where we were used to soft ocean breezes. Emi got a fever which was daunting and would not give way to normal body temperature.

I went to the camp canteen located two barracks away to get ice to cool her down and reduce her fever. No hospital or physician in any organized fashion yet.

So, each day, I made a nuisance of myself pleading with the canteen manager or subordinate for ice and finally after several weeks, Emi's fever broke and stabilized. I thought that Emi, my mother, was a goner because the fever persisted. So, when the fever broke, I was overjoyed. No more visits to the canteen for ice.

## JOBS IN CAMP

Morizo helped himself to be a mess hall cook with primary responsibility for cooking large vats of rice (*gohan*). When the rice was cooked, it laid a crust around the vat. That crust was what many of us coveted because with a little salt or *umeboshi* (pickled plum), it was a meal, a fine, tasty meal, better than what was being served to block inmates.

My job was to help with the block library. I always liked to read and write; therefore, the library was an ideal place for me to work.

## LIFE IN CAMP

During the hot summer months, the winds swept through camp taking the dust and sand with it. Since the barracks were not completed, the wind blew through the tar paper around the barrack and penetrated the wall to make breathing difficult.

After the first summer, in 1942, the winds were less of a problem. Water hosed around the barrack kept dust and whirling sand to a minimum. Later, open spaces between and around the barracks were filled with plants, or in front of our barrack, Yutaka and Morizo worked on creating a rock garden in a landscaped waterfall filled fish pond. They attracted others in the block to help with projects that beautified the block.

Adjacent to our barrack was the camp police unit, the quartermaster office for distribution of clothing and equipment to inmates, and the block manager's office. Morizo was our Block 28 manager and therefore, attended the camp-wide block manager's meetings.

Running through the center of Poston Camp 1 was a canal. It flowed near our block. Therefore, during the hot summer months, it was an ideal hole to dip or even swim because it was widened at the spot close to our barrack.

In Fall 1942, school started. In addition to going to public school, I went to private Japanese language classes. In finishing the eighth grade, I walked to Block 30 and beyond. For senior high school, I had to walk from Block 28 through Block 27 to go beyond Block 26. Classes were held in adobe buildings that were quite cool in the hot weather and cold in the winter months.

In a way, education in camp was a farce. It was wartime. What and where were the teachers? The *hakujin* teachers were mainly from America's heartland or East Coast. One of my favorites was Riley, a teacher from Indiana. He wrote some beautiful poetry. One teacher whom I still remember was whom I think of as "Gravel Gertie," a heavyset "grandmotherly type" who looked like a prune-faced character from a comic strip.

Poston had several outstanding Nisei teachers. Sanematsu in drafting class. Igauye in commercial classes such as typewriting, communication, and English. But, in some classes such as algebra, geometry, or trigonometry, it was "Here is your textbook, do all problems and turn in paperwork." In some courses, this freewheeling approach was coveted because I could work through the problems, and even bankroll a few nickels in the process. I liked my Mathematics and Science (Chemistry and Physics) courses.

Outside of the public school, Morizo sent me to a Japanese calligraphy teacher. I learned much about *shuji*, using brushstrokes to write Chinese characters. All the while, I learned how to read and write the Japanese language.

## EARLY CAMP EVENTS

Life in Poston in the 1942 year was chaotic inasmuch as the living quarters were yet to be finished. News of Japan's victories in their quest for their Greater Prosperity Sphere was advancing. Morizo and others got access to shortwave broadcasts, printed the news on mimeograph machines, and told youngsters like me to distribute the news. But as the war continued and the Battle of Midway was fought, the tide of battle changed from Japan's victories to Japan's defeats. No longer were youngsters like me distributing newsletters of what was captured from shortwave broadcasts, but the distribution of the camp paper, the *Poston Chronicle*, held forth, articles written by a cadre of professionals.

## POSTON RIOTS

In November 1942, the Poston Riots became news. It was happening in the open area between Block 28, our block, and the canal, in a community building. I saw an angry group of Poston inmates whom I was told were mainly Kibei who charged Saburo Kido, JACL president, with pro-America statements and wanted to "sabotage" him. After all, JACL was originally formed by Nisei and did not welcome the Kibei crowd. This incident placed a cloud on camp life as well as the governance process going forward.

## THE LOYALTY QUESTIONNAIRE

The pause for military recruits from Poston took place with the administering the so-called "loyalty" questionnaire in Spring 1943. America needed soldiers. The questionnaire forced a dividing line in families and friends. The "no-no", the "yes-no", the "no-yes," and "yes-yes" responses triggered adults being sent to different venues.

The "no-no" boys like the Okabeppu brothers, Hayato, Akira and Takeshi, were sent to Tule Lake Segregation Camp in California's northern border near the Oregon state line. Yutaka's son Archie joined his cousins. I was still fourteen and therefore, did not have to respond to the questionnaire. But, I thought that my father, Morizo, had a change of heart due to the questionnaires and no longer harbored any thoughts of returning to Japan even though he was not an American citizen, but a Japanese citizen.

As the war continued, Hayato Okabeppu and Archie Fujimoto were sent to the Santa Fe, New Mexico, to a camp administered by the US Department of Justice. Akira and Takeshi Okabeppu were interned at Fort Lincoln in Bismarck, North Dakota.

The so-called "loyalty" questionnaires divided families, caused disruptions in family life, and in some cases, caused considerable friction.

Grace and I later, in 2009, visited the New Mexico and Fort Lincoln sites to see the location of incarceration. We also queried Archie and the Okabeppu brothers about life in these segregated camps and through these interviews concluded that I was most fortunate to be of an age where I stayed in Poston for the entire four years of being an inmate in one of America's concentration camps.

Jack Fujimoto

## THE HOT SUMMER MONTHS AND COLD WINTER MONTHS

The summer months were hot in the desert country. Morizo had me order a "swamp cooler" from one of the catalog sales, Speigel's, Sears, or Montgomery Ward, that I installed in the front window of our barrack. The water trickling through the mesh in the cooler provided considerable comfort.

Also, Morizo had me cut a chunk of wood from the floor such that we could crawl down into the ground where it was considerably cooler than the room. These are ways in which the barracks were livable during the summer.

In the cold winter months, Morizo, as block manager, prevailed upon the camp quartermaster in the room adjacent to his office to provide "pee" coats to inmates. In addition to clothing, we devised the use of gallon cans filled with charcoal to keep us warm. The gallon cans were pierced to provide holes for heat dissipating and a wire carrying handle to keep us warm while walking. Often, we used these warmers while we watched movies or shows in the open air.

## JUDO

Judo practice under Hagio Sensei was held at 5 a.m. in Block 39 dojo (practice hall). In winter months, Morizo got me up early because he went to the block mess hall for rice cooking. I went to the dojo where there was usually a large fifty-gallon drum with wood burning that heated us up. Archie, my cousin, and I along with John Saito often practiced in these early morning practice sessions.

In tournaments, I was strong enough to wade through opponents to earn a *shodan* (first degree) black belt. After leaving Poston, I never took up judo again.

## SUMO

I also took up sumo because the Kariya brothers in Block 28 were an inspiration. Masashi (Mush) and Yoneo Kariya along with their father were my teachers. The epitome of my success was when we visited Poston Camp 2 for a tournament and in the "take 5 opponents out" tournament, I got four of them to fall; however, I lost to the fifth opponent, but yet, got a trophy. That was the extent of my sumo experience.

## SPORTS

Otherwise, I participated in various Poston camp leagues in basketball, football, and softball. Morizo often attended these games to push me to do well in sports. Later, I learned that I suffered from a pulmonary function that prevented me from being a "super" athlete, often winded.

## BLOCK MANAGER

*Morizo is in the center of the second row of block managers in Poston Camp 1.*

Morizo attended the monthly meetings of block managers. He was the liaison between the Poston camp administration and the block inmates. Morizo had the time because his job as mess hall rice cooking usually ended in early morning.

The work of block manager did not appear to be a strenuous or stressful job because he was always available to help his brother, Yutaka, in his beautification campaign for Block 28. Morizo recruited volunteers to help Yutaka dig a pond in Block 28, build a bridge, go to the Colorado River to stock the pond with turtles (*suppon*) and carp fish (*koi*), and gather boulders to build a waterfall.

Yutaka was a master craftsman and landscape architect.

*Yutaka engaged many Block 28 inmates to help him design the rock garden.*

*The group of Block 28 volunteers who helped with the rock garden and fountain, all in the name of beautifying the block. Morizo is on the right sitting on a rock.*

One of the humorous stories told by some of the younger teens was that the man on the left had "balls" (testicles) that were bigger than a "softball." Since there was no privacy in the lavatories, kids would come and gawk at the strange size which was possible because there were no dividers between lavatory stools.

*One of the prides of Block 28 was the bridge and pond that Yutaka designed and supervised its construction. The pond was the repository of fish and turtles from the Colorado River.*

Jack Fujimoto

## FISHING IN THE COLORADO RIVER

Morizo went with Yutaka to fish the Colorado River. The riverbank was within walking distance. Yutaka was an avid fisherman. Morizo was less so.

Yutaka's son, Archie, and I often went to the river where we caught turtles and carp. There might be an occasional perch or bass, but that was a rare catch. The swift running water of the Colorado River was a sight to behold. The relatively stagnant section of the river was usually on our side and so, when we got thirsty and needed a swig, we had to be careful that the stagnant side was clear of cow dung and tree branches.

*Mrs. Niiro, holding Seiko, Yutaka's youngest daughter, was most grateful to Yutaka for his catch of turtles.*

Turtles were coveted by inmates in Block 28. Mrs. Niiro in the barrack adjacent to us drank the blood of turtles to recover from some rheumatoid illness, so it was reported to Yutaka. So, Yutaka had a mission to catch and bring turtles back to Block 28.

Carp was not very tasty and therefore, not very eagerly welcomed. They swam well in the block pond that Yutaka designed.

## BLOCK 28 CRAFTS WORK

Yutaka used his crafts and carpenter talent to make brooches and pins for clothing ornaments in his spare time. He used the mesquite tree branches or other desert plants to design bird pins for women to put on their clothes. Some paint, some glue, a pin, and he had a gift for some lucky lady.

In that way, Yutaka was much more into the crafts and talents than Morizo who did well in his block manager role.

*Pictured are many inmates of Block 28. Morizo is in first row with son, Takashi, on his lap. Yutaka is in second row holding his characteristic fishing pole.*

## OTHER REMEMBRANCES

When we remodeled the Encinitas home on several occasions, we lost many photographs. It does not do justice with these few remnants of photographs of the "rich" life lived in a concentration camp; however, each can elicit a story of how each person captured a part of Poston culture.

Jack Fujimoto

## SOME TAKEAWAYS
## EMI AND IKEBANA

Emi was fortunate to go to the Poston Flower Arrangement School for two years and get her diploma. This surely could not have happened from prior experiences.

*Pictured is a certificate issued to Emi Fujimoto for completing a two-year course in Ikenobo flower arrangement (ikebana).*

## BLOCK 28 RESIDENTS

There was a lot of talent among the Block 28 residents.

Obviously, Yutaka was a leader in designing and building a large pond with carp and turtles.

The teachers of sumo like the Kariya family patriarch and his two sons, Mush and Yoneo were mainstays who practiced on a *dohyo* in the block. Judo had Hagio as one of its teachers and we practiced in nearby Block 39.

The Hosaka brothers, Fred and John, lived in the block, but we very seldomly encountered any activity with them. Their patriarch, Minetaro, was segregated in Santa Fe and later, in Lordsburg, as described in Fred's book. Fred made no comment in his book about Morizo being his block manager. I wondered why?

The Okabeppu brothers who left Encinitas with us departed for Tule Lake segregated concentration camp as a result of their "no-no" response to the camp-wide loyalty questionnaire. There, Hayato was then dispatched to Santa Fe (NM) segregation and Akira and Takeshi were to Bismarck, North Dakota, another US Department of Justice camp.

My cousin, Archie Fujimoto, just eighteen, also got shipped away, not to Tule Lake but to Santa Fe camp for segregated aliens where he joined his cousin.

*Pictured are Hayato and Akira Okabeppu in a photograph taken in 2000, many years after they returned to their Kagoshima roots in 1946. They helped Yutaka and Morizo in the Poston camp projects until they were evicted to go to Tule Lake segregation camp in 1943 because of their responses to the loyalty questionnaire.*

*This is Takeshi Okabeppu, the younger brother of Hayato and Akira, who repatriated to Kagoshima, Japan, with them. Picture was taken by me while he was in the hospital.*

*Pictured are sisters, cousins, and friends from Poston.*

*Pictured are Akiko, unknown friend, and Yasuko Kajihara who often chummed together in Poston camp. Akiko is my cousin.*

# MORIZO LEAVES POSTON – 1945

Poston, one of the ten War Relocation Authority (WRA) camps, also known as America's concentration camps, was to close with the others in November 1945.

Morizo decided to take his family out of Poston in October 1945, with a paltry twenty-five dollars offered by the American government. He hired a truck to take what he could along with the family: Emi and the five kids. Eiko Kay was born later after returning from Poston to Encinitas. We went to one of the labor camps that Yutaka had before being evacuated in 1942 and one that still stood there managed by Eugene Ben Vau, the German who bought the farm from Yutaka. Due to the 1913 California Alien Land Law, Yutaka did not own the property that Ben Vau farmed, but Ben Vau bought the strawberry farm.

## SHORT-LIVED STAY AT BEN VAU LABOR CAMP

After a short stay at the labor camp, Morizo and Yutaka decided to lease some property adjacent to the Ben Vau labor camp. Since the brothers were to do sharecrop operations with Ben Vau on his leased hilltop in La Costa, they took some used lumber from Ben Vau and built a small house in a valley near La Costa Boulevard and present-day Interstate Highway 5 (I-5 freeway). The Ben Vau farm in La Costa was about ten miles away and featured the cultivation and harvesting of tomatoes.

## BUILDING A NEW HOUSE WITH YUTAKA

Our new home was built by Morizo and Yutaka with help from Archie and me. It was two houses linked with a common roof but had a space between the two houses that could accommodate a garage. We had separate outhouses and bath facilities inasmuch as Morizo liked his bath, much more that Yutaka.

It was built in a valley where pre-World War II (1941 and before), we often went there to pick up the dry lima beans that were left after the initial harvest had been done. By hand, we sifted through the vines to pick the smaller beans. Our mothers, Emi and Hisayo, boiled the beans with sugar to make a sweet bean paste that they often folded into a bean cake, a holiday delicacy, *mochi manju*.

The new house was under two large sycamore trees adjacent to a shallow creek whose water flowed to Baniquitos Slough in a heavy rain.

Flocks of chickens were cultured and laid eggs for us to consume. I had a pig, named Herman, whom I received as a pet. By the time that I left the farm in 1946, I parted with Herman and I learned later that Herman went to a slaughterhouse to adorn someone's dinner plate. I liked animals, but I suspect that Morizo did not care much either way.

## SHARECROPPERS

Morizo did sharecropping with Eugene Ben Vau from November 1945 to November 1948, a period of three years. Due to the 1913 California Alien Land Law, Morizo, not being an American citizen could not purchase real property. But in 1948, Morizo negotiated with Bondy on the southside of Encinitas to buy some five acres of property in my name inasmuch as I was an American citizen. The purchase was made and Morizo's sharecropping experience came to an end.

## SHARECROPPING EXPERIENCES

During the sharecropping days, there were some interesting experiences.

The tomatoes and other vegetables were grown on a large hilltop in La Costa. The land had to be tilled. In that first year of 1945 to 1946, I recall that I did much of the tractor work to plow and disk the land for planting and later, adding manure.

I had a hectic schedule at age seventeen. My high school credits for graduation from San Dieguito High School was three "solids" shy and so, my counselor, Mrs. Elizabeth Brass, gave me books to study, and later, examined my knowledge of those courses. I passed.

I also wanted to letter in interscholastic football in the fall season of 1945. George Pratt was the football coach. He came from the East Coast and did not know much about West Coast prejudice against Japanese incarceration into wartime camps. He welcomed me to play football and often took me close to my home because I had to practice beyond the bus hours.

On the days that I could get home early, I grabbed a *takuwan* sandwich (two slices of bread with a pickled daikon in between) and drove to the La Costa hilltop to drive the tractor until 9 p.m.

After football season, I did not try out for basketball at San Dieguito High School, but I did try out for the baseball season. I played varsity second base and third base in the spring of 1946, and at the end of the season, got my letterman sweater and initiation into the San Dieguito High School Letterman Club.

For basketball, I occasionally went back to Encinitas and played with the JANELs (Japanese American Nikkei of Encinitas and Leucadia), a local community support group that featured several activities, several of which were held at the local hamburger stand in Ponto, just off Highway 101. The stand was run by a *hakujin* older man who befriended the Nikkei of our area.

All the while, I continued to work the sharecropped farm.

To grow the crops at the La Costa hilltop, water had to be pumped from a well at the base of the hill. The hydraulic system was started and stopped at the end of the irrigation. A by-product of that operation required me to visit the pump. In that area were many frogs, large enough that I caught some and learned how to grill their legs for a tasty meal.

On the other hand, there were rattlers around that we had to catch, skin, and dry, later grinding and mixing with chicken feed to feed those chickens that were slightly ailing or limping. It perked them up. Must have been "strong stuff."

## NO MORE SHARECROPPING WORK FOR ME

In June 1946, I graduated from San Dieguito High School in a senior class of thirty students. I knew many of them prior to World War II and pre-evacuation days. Guys like Badger and Briggs from the Rancho Santa Fe Estates. Pugh who graduated with honors. Largent, Cleary, Ben Nakata, Nieman, and Rea from athletics competition. Girls, I did not know much. And I do not recall any Latinos.

It was at this time that I really appreciated Morizo's words. He understood how difficult it was to farm, especially sharecropping. On the other hand, he knew that he relied on the oldest son and by tradition, the oldest carries on the name and work of the father. Well, on graduation, he lifted any obligation that I follow in his footsteps. "I was liberated." I told him that I wanted to pursue a college education. His only admonishment was that he would not provide any financial support. I understood. Morizo had a family to feed.

## BILL YOKOYAMA, A COUSIN

Bill was a favored cousin. He helped Morizo and Emi in many ways. In agriculture, Bill had a green thumb. He could grow crops, sell them, and eventually, ship them to all parts of the United States and into some foreign markets. In later years, I was his best man at his wedding. That is how favored I was.

One of the first persons befriending me to get into academics was my cousin, Bill Yokoyama. Later, Bill becomes a catalyst for Morizo to switch from growing truck crops to the farming of flowers that eventually led to Morizo being able to retire from farming.

Bill was Nihei Yokoyama's third son and a flower grower. Nihei was related to Emi and befriended her when she returned to America. Nihei and Bill lived in Rosemead in the San Gabriel

Valley off of Earle Street in some rehabilitated Quonset huts that were declared surplus by the United States Navy.

Bill befriended me and invited me to stay with him since I wanted to enroll at Pasadena City College and his house was fairly close to the college. I found a "schoolboy" job in Altadena with a chiropractor who had just remarried with his wife having two small sons.

Bill had flowers growing in several places. One of his parcels was in leased land adjacent to where Morizo was farming after buying his land on Westfield Drive (Birmingham Drive today) in 1948.

Bill did not feature carnations as much as he grew beautiful mums, daisies, and jips. He also introduced dried pussy willows that lasted several years. Bill, although craved a college education in civil engineering, did do well in flower growing.

## TRAGEDY HAPPENS, YUTAKA DIES

Pictured is Yutaka, Morizo's older brother, who played a prominent part of our lives.

In spring 1947, while working as a "schoolboy" in Altadena and going to the West Campus of Pasadena City College (John Muir College), I learned that Yutaka was working on Eugene Ben Vau's house in Leucadia and had a carpentry accident. Being rushed to a La Jolla Hospital, he lost much blood and died.

I wanted to attend the funeral but Morizo said that I should focus on my studies and excused me from the funeral. I realized then that Morizo had his hands full. He was now the patriarch of the Fujimoto clan in America with Yutaka's passing. Grandfather Yasukichi would not be able to come to America anymore at his advanced age.

Archie, the only son of the Yutaka family, would need to have Morizo's counsel and support, since they lived in the same area but in different homes. In a way, Morizo could rely on Archie much more than me, Archie being twenty-one years of age, and just getting back his American citizenship that he lost when he went into the Tule Lake segregation camp and Santa Fe Department of Justice camp. I was eighteen at the time.

In hindsight, it was fortuitous that the accidental passing of Yutaka gave Morizo the opportunity to work with Archie, a sort of adopted son since I was no longer around the premises. Archie was a tremendous help to Morizo.

Archie and Akiko referred with affection to Morizo as *otchan*. I do not know whether that is a contraction of some Japanese terms, but that is what Morizo was called.

## ENCINITAS COMMUNITY CENTER

When Morizo returned to Encinitas, he found that the pre-World War II Encinitas Japanese Community Center was looted.

There was nothing that we could take back. Such terrible things can happen during wartime hysteria.

## NO ASSETS, A NEW BEGINNING

Even Reynoso, our hired hand before evacuating to Poston camp, reaped the profits from the spring "bumper" cucumber crop and evacuated our "old" house, neither of which gave any thanks to Morizo. No cucumber crop sharing of profits or return of the "old" house.

Also, of the several thousand dollars that Morizo had deposited in his account pre-World War II with Yokohama Specie Bank, Morizo got only a pittance of the several thousand dollars in return.

In essence, Morizo had to start from scratch to develop a financial base. But, he must have been good at it inasmuch as he continually avoided debt and was finally able to buy his real property in Encinitas.

## NEIGHBORS

In the Loibl compound that existed adjacent to the land that Morizo and Hayato had developed prior to World War II came the Furukawa family after the end of World War II. Morizo did not know them well; however, Shiro Furukawa, the second son in their family was about my age at the time. I got to know him for a brief time and thus, Morizo got to know them in the 1945–1948 time frame.

Shiro had friends in Pasadena. He took me on one occasion to meet the Miyamoto family, one girl in the family that he was dating. That was the occasion that piqued my interest in attending Pasadena City College if the opportunity ever arose.

After the Furukawa family left the Loibl compound, the Taniguchi family moved into the separate Loibl quarters. Their family was related in some distant fashion to Hisayo, wife of Yutaka. As I recall, there were four children along with parents. "Stump" Taniguchi, one of two boys in the family, became a well-known jockey in horse racing circles.

Another neighbor was the Horiba family. They moved from Mesa, Arizona, to start a small farming operation near the Ben Vau farm. Masa, Taka, and Sabe Horiba, along with parents, mainly grew tomatoes. They farmed a short period of time, soon moving to Los Angeles. Morizo got to know of them. I got to know them much better because Taka, one of the sons, strutted around in his new Studebaker car that he said that he won at a raffle or some event.

Anyway, it was a major shift in automotive design where it was difficult to identify which end of the car was the front and which end was the rear. It was designed by Loewy. Taka was proud of the car and showed it around. At that time, the JANEL organization (Japanese American Nikkei of Encinitas and Leucadia) was formed. Mas Horiba was one of its founders, along with Bill Yoshida whose parents lived in Encinitas. Taka showed off his car to the organization. There were only a handful of Nikkei living in the Encinitas, Leucadia area; however, there was a high level of camaraderie. It was one way of Morizo and Emi socializing among their peers.

## RESETTLEMENT LESSONS

During the years after leaving Poston camp, resettlement in our prior community was a short breather for Morizo to get his family back into place. Mom gave birth to our last member of the Fujimoto family, a daughter, who survives as Eiko Kay Fujimoto.

Finances were a problem. In addition to sharecropping in La Costa for Ben Vau, I went to work when opportunity presented itself to help Ellsworth with his avocado groves. Every one of his many trees needed a sulfur treatment to bear better fruit.

The accidental passing of Yutaka posed additional burdens for our two families. Having Archie available to help Morizo, I know, was a tremendous help. After all, I was a college schoolboy with no income.

# MORIZO AS ENTREPRENEUR

In 1948, Morizo and Emi used my name to purchase a parcel of land in the south side of Encinitas, bordering on Cardiff-by-the-Sea. They shed their sharecropping experience to start farming on their own again.

Since Morizo knew how to grow vegetables, that is what he started. I recall his growing bountiful crops of pole tomatoes, cucumbers, peppers, and squash. It was tedious, tiring, and yet, quite a gamble in that such farming depended so much on the elements, weather, the quality of seed, irrigation, nutrients, and labor.

Emi also figured into the mix, working in the field, packing the produce, besides cooking and providing a home.

## BILL YOKOYAMA GREW FLOWERS

Bill Yokoyama, our cousin, grew flowers on leased land adjacent to where Morizo farmed. He brought his trailer home and parked it in the valley adjacent to the house. He had his father, Nihei Yokoyama, stay in the trailer and monitor Bill's farm of leased land where flowers grew. In this way, Bill supported Nihei who was still responsible for the remainder of his family of Masako, Bob, and Yoshiko. Bill's older brothers, George and Harry, were busy with their families and Bill was still single.

Bill was a multitasker who grew flowers, trucked them to market, and sold flowers on the Wall Street Flower Exchange in Los Angeles.

Bill ranched at several parcels, including one in Duarte and later, Santa Paula in Ventura County. His specialties, as I recall, were mums and daisies. He was not much for carnations. But, Bill convinced Morizo to switch from vegetables, truck crops, to grow flowers, especially carnations.

At that time, Tak Muto from the San Fernando Valley, one of Bill's acquaintances, moved to Encinitas across the street from Morizo's farm, and started a flower-shipping operation. Tak Muto established a shipping cooperative with several flower growers. This eventually grew to become a well-known cooperative such that flowers were advertised as coming from the "the gold coast" where quality flowers, especially carnations, were grown.

Moving from truck farming of vegetables to flowers was a profitable move for Morizo. Initial investment in plastic hothouses was costly; however, the "bottom line" was a profit that was not seen in producing vegetables for the Los Angeles produce market.

## FLOWER GROWING WAS A FAMILY ENTERPRISE

Soon after the farm property of five acres was bought, an additional seven acres was bought. Plastic houses for growing flowers were built on much of the acreage. In later years, some of the property was leased to nurseries such as the palm tree nursery who kept many palm trees there. Transactions may have been limited but still required large areas for the potted trees.

Morizo and Emi, along with Tak, Judy, and Eiko provided much of the labor inasmuch as I had gone into the academic world and later, in 1948, into voluntary military service. Fumie and Yoko also left to pursue their academic careers.

Since I left the family in 1946, I was less involved with Morizo becoming involved in the growing of carnations as a cash crop and his work with the Muto cooperative. But, I do know that it was a successful transition in wealth building.

## ON THE HOME FRONT

After graduating from John Muir College in Pasadena with an Associate in Arts degree in June 1948, and successfully passing qualifications for guaranteeing a seat in the University of California, Berkeley, School of Engineering, I visited the farm to help in furnishing the new home being built for the Fujimoto family. I believe that Tom Hayward, neighbor and architect, helped with the design and layout of the house.

I recall taking some lumber and making a dining nook that included a place for Morizo to sit with Emi on the other side. This dining nook included a drawer for rice storage. This dining nook must have been a treasured piece of furniture because for many years, Morizo sat there, ate his *chazuke,* drank his milk with Twinkies at night before bedtime, and played his solitaire card games.

I only spent two months at our new home before joining Sabe Horiba, a former neighbor, to volunteer to serve in the United States Army. Sabe was interested in the medical field and I was interested in the Intelligence field.

So, we got inducted in San Diego, got on a train with a *hakujin* friend, Paul Watt, to go to Fort Ord in Monterey, California, for basic training.

In 1949, I believe that Fumie left home to go to Kaiser Hospital Nursing Program in Piedmont, California, in the San Francisco Bay area. Fumie related to me that the years before leaving for higher education were difficult years for her because Morizo denied her from enjoying dates and dances, especially at the high school. Maybe it was because he did not want his daughters socializing much and keeping academics in their radar screen.

Yoko left home to go to Pasadena for further education.

So, in essence, the new family of Morizo and Emi, along with Tak, Judy, and Eiko did the work of growing flowers. They also helped with construction and decorating the new house.

In July 1952, when I got honorably discharged from the US Army (DD 214), I went to the Fujimoto homestead only to spend a couple of months before leaving again, this time to go to UCLA, for my junior year of academic work.

I did some work in the carnation plastic houses, especially in taking the flowers to the Muto Cooperative Station, where I met Tak Muto, along with my cousin, Archie, and Hayashi and Minamide. Nemoto might have been doing some business with the cooperative at that time too.

It was a difficult time of life for Archie. His father got killed in a freak accident in 1947. His being the only son, he had to help his mother and her farming activities. So, often, he confided in Morizo and for a period of time, as I recall, she was involved with the Muto Cooperative venture. Their farm on Saxony Drive in Encinitas produced some outstanding flowers.

## OUR NEW HOME IN 1948

The new home was built on a knoll that had a fabulous view of the Pacific Ocean when we looked south. We could see much of La Jolla on a clear day. I thought that it was fantastic and rather inspirational.

Morizo could look out of the backyard for the Pacific Ocean view. On the front side, he could see the other flower growers with their plastic houses. To the side of the house, he made his *furoba* (his bathhouse) and placed it in such a way that any wind might help him burn the papers and twigs to heat up the tub faster.

No longer did we have to dig a trench or hole for an outhouse. We had indoor plumbing with flushing toilets leading to leech lines to the north of the house. Those lines gave us some difficulties later when they got clogged and needed to be rerouted. That is when we thought it might be better to explore joining a sewage system such as the Cardiff Sanitation District.

Morizo liked his fruit trees. So, when I went home, I enjoyed eating some of the exotic tropical fruits such as sapota, cherimoya, guava, and banana. Also, he had many citrus trees growing producing oranges, kumquats, and grapefruits.

As time went on, he put in a pond much like the one that was in front of our Poston concentration camp barrack. No fish, only rocks and miniature trees.

Annually, I went home during my years at UCLA, to help Morizo with his income tax filing. I would collate records and do the family's filing. From these reports, I could see that he was having a profit in the bottom line and saving. He was following the mantra of "take no debt" much as he had preached to me during my early years.

## VISIT OF SEITOKU

*Picture shows Seitoku Katako on the right with his older brother, Makoto Kubo. Seitoku was adopted by the Katako family. Seitoku returned to Japan after his American experience to work a lifetime for Japan's Ministry of Agriculture.*

The Japanese government negotiated a plan to train young Japanese students to come to the United States to learn agricultural methods.

In 1960, Seitoku Katako, a nephew of my mother, applied and was accepted to come to the United States to learn about growing vegetables and flowers. He was assigned to Morizo for his tutelage. In essence, though, rather than Morizo showing Seitoku the finer points of growing and harvesting, Archie took over the task. Archie was a "big-time" pole tomato grower and more Seitoku's age, and so, they worked together quite well.

Archie was like a surrogate son of Morizo and spoke the Japanese language well. Calling Morizo, *otchan* was a friendly gesture of respect for Morizo by Archie. After all, I was seldom home and therefore, it was much more practical that Morizo rely upon Archie for advice and help. I did not mind it at all.

## BECOMING AN AMERICAN

In 1952, the United States Congress passed the Walter-McCarran naturalization legislation that permitted Issei to become naturalized citizens. Sus Uyeda and I joined a group of Issei in the Venice and West Los Angeles area in 1953 at Braddock Elementary School to teach a citizenship course, the United States Constitution, some history of the US, and what to expect on a naturalization test.

I do not know where Morizo and Emi did their citizenship preparation or where and when they took their test, but I do recall Morizo saying that they were naturalized and voted Republican. They liked Ronald Reagan as governor and later, president.

Jolene, in her interview with Emi, inquired about her *baachan* (Emi's reference as grandmother) voting Republican every election, she was told that her *baachan* did not vote Republican always like Morizo. She read much as time became more and more available.

Jack Fujimoto

## TRIP TO ARKANSAS

*Pictured is Morizo on the back porch of our motel in Fayetteville, Arkansas. The humid weather was to be overcome by winds that hit our motel daily.*

Grace and I got married in 1956. Crystal and Randall were born in our second five-year plan. When I got a National Science Foundation scholarship to attend the University of Arkansas in 1964, I took the family to Fayetteville, Arkansas, the home of the "soowey hog."

In August 1964, I finished my graduate course and planned to drive back to Los Angeles with the family.

Morizo decided that he wanted to come to Arkansas to see the landscape, join us for the ride back, and learn something about

Arkansas culture. We took him to a catfish farm. He also went to Sam Walton's office in Bentonville, Arkansas, just outside the university. We exposed him to Eureka Springs where hillbilly music from the Ozarks was heard. But the one thing that he cherished most was a "bite" into a head of lettuce, saying that he wanted his greens and some crunchiness . . . iceberg lettuce filled his need.

On the drive back to Los Angeles, I took Morizo and family to Truman's Independence Library, the Eisenhower home in Abilene, Kansas, and to a Denver hospital where we had Crystal examined for a medical problem.

*Pictured is Morizo at the Eisenhower home in Kansas along with Grace, Crystal, and Randall.*

Being that Morizo was a Republican, it was appropriate that I stop and have him pictured.

## MORIZO AND HIS CADILLAC

In the late 1950s, Morizo often talked about owning a large car, such as a Cadillac. He bought one. It was a DeVille, one of the larger ones.

In the early 1960s, I drove the Deville on some trips to Northern California. One trip was to Lassen National Park where some of us slept in the car while, I recall, I slept on a large log.

Another trip involved going to the Sequoia National Park near Fresno. There, the kids could frolic in the cool river waters with grandparents looking after them.

Another trip was a visit to Lake Tahoe. On that trip, Judy's kids, Sachi and Tam, joined us.

We enjoyed our drive to Poston concentration camp.

All these adventures involved Morizo's use of the Cadillac. The Cadillac at the time was a huge car, but through the ages, it had been designed for a smaller clientele. I drove Morizo's Cadillac often and liked its comfort and performance. I owned one personally for twenty years.

## TED AND JUDY TOOK OVER THE FARM IN 1967. MORIZO AND EMI WENT INTO RETIREMENT.

*Morizo at Sequoia National Park with Crystal and Randall.*

*Grace lets Crystal and Randall play in the creek at the park.*

*Jolene with her cousins, Sachi and Tam, at Lake Tahoe.*

*Enjoying Lake Tahoe in rented rowboat.*

*Morizo with Emi and the growing family.*

# SPIRITUAL COMMUNITY

## MORIZO, HIS SPIRITUAL SIDE

Living in Encinitas, it was difficult to cultivate his spiritual aspect of his life. Morizo and Emi got literature on a routine basis from Seicho No Ie, a religious group. They attended some sessions of the Meshiya Kyo. But, Morizo and Emi wanted to keep their ties to the Buddhist temple. So, they helped to form the Encinitas Kyudo Kai with the help of Reverend Koju Terada from the Buddhist Temple of San Diego.

## SEICHO NO IE (RELIGIOUS GROUP)

Seicho No Ie was a religious group founded by Masaharu Taniguchi. What I knew of the religion was that it combined the many great values in some existing religions and other mortal values. The group had a monthly magazine that was read by Emi, less by Morizo, but I do not know that either attended any of their services. There was no Seicho No Ie temple in the Encinitas area. They also subscribed to a newsletter from Seicho No Ie, a religious order with its headquarters in Los Angeles.

## MESSIAH GROUP (MESHIYA KYO)

Feeling that they had super healing powers in their hands, Morizo and Emi attended sessions of the Messiah Group along with Yukie Ito, Yutaka's daughter, and her husband. As I recall, they met at some facility in Vista just north of Encinitas.

Morizo would take his hand and hold it over a body part that had pain and over a time, the pain went away. He told me that I have that power and therefore, I should use it to help the body overcome pain. I did not have any success and therefore, concluded that I did not have that power. Grace said that she did not have this type of power; however, she could sit on rocks in Sedona, Arizona, and say that the vibrations that she felt healed her pains. So, I suspect that everyone either has some supernatural powers or not.

## TRANSMIGRATION, CLAIRVOYENT MESSAGES

Tam Matsumoto, granddaughter to Morizo and Emi, occasionally writes to me about her clairvoyant type of encounter with *Jiichan* and *Baachan* as she calls them.

Recently, she wrote about her chance discovery of their visit from Amida Land in a 2021 New Year's mailing to me. She wrote that *Jiichan* was here to observe his six children, spending time with each one before he was to undertake another activity starting the 2021 year with *Baachan* and others.

Strange that I never realized *Jiichan*'s presence if he were present. After all, *Jiichan* passed his earthly life in 1994 and *Baachan* in 1989.

In previous messages from Tam, some interesting tales emerged. *Baachan*, at one time, was *Jiichan*'s teacher. They were not in their earthly roles as husband and wife.

In another message, *Jiichan* apologized to his earthly children that he treated us the way that he was treated as he grew up in Hiroshima, Japan . . . nothing violent but verbal and into the woodshed.

In another message, *Jiichan* was interested in his biography that I was thinking of writing and that I finally wrote sketchily.

## ENCINITAS KYUDO KAI

When Reverend Koju Terada was resident minister of the Buddhist Temple of San Diego (BTSD), my parents, Morizo and Emi Fujimoto, along with some other Jodo Shinshu Buddhists in the Encinitas area prevailed upon Reverend Terada to establish a fellowship (*Kyudo Kai*)( 求道会 ) in Encinitas. Being some thirty-five miles from BTSD, it was difficult for them to hear the Dharma (messages of the Buddha from ordained ministers) on a consistent basis. So, thanks to the generosity of Reverend Terada, they were able to engage him for a monthly visit in the 1970s.

## ROTATING VENUE

During the 1970s, occasionally, I took my family from Los Angeles to visit my parents in Encinitas. These were sporadic visits because I was a ranking administrator in the Los Angeles Community College District and later, president of Sacramento City College. From time to time those came after a Kyudo Kai meeting at their home. They seemed happiest from those meetings and shared the leftover refreshments with Grace and me along with our four children. It must have been something extra because one of the virtues practiced by Emi was to be generous to others. So, she went out of her way to have sushi, some traditional Japanese delicacies and liquids. For farming families, the role of the mother of the house was not easy. For special occasions such as Kyudo Kai and the several visitors, much preparation was necessary.

All of this is written to express our appreciation to Emi showing how much we observed in doing things that showed the best of the Fujimoto name.

## REVEREND KOJU TERADA

Over the past eight decades, I have been associated with various aspects of Buddhism in America. Early days involved going to learn the Japanese language at the BTSD as well as accompanying my father, Morizo, in his temple events in the 1930s. During WW II and Poston Concentration Camp era, I attended the Buddhist temple services. After serving in the Korean Conflict as a GI in East Asia operations, I commenced teaching Dharma school at West Los Angeles Temple along with BSA Sangha Award students. In the 1980s, I became chairman of the board of Trustees for Institute of Buddhist Studies in Berkeley for a dozen years. It is from this perspective that I share my admiration for ministers such as Reverend Koju Terada who go out of their way to share the Dharma with interested persons like my parents.

Personally, I liked to listen to Dharma messages from Rev. Bunyu Fujimura of the WLABT in the 1950s and 1960s.

## MORIZO AND EMI PUBLICATIONS FUND

When I was chairman of the board of Trustees for the Institute of Buddhist Studies (IBS) in Berkeley, California, starting in 1984, I realized that Morizo and Emi were reading much religious literature. Since the Institute was looking to connect its graduate school courses to its neighboring Graduate Theological Union (GTU) (for transferability of its courses of study), it was my thought that the Institute would benefit more by providing funds for IBS scholarly publications rather than scholarship grants. And so, the Board ratified the establishment of the Morizo and Emi Fujimoto Publications Fund.

Its establishment also honored Morizo and Emi to promote their interest in reading Buddhist literature.

# MORIZO IN RETIREMENT

In 1967, Ted and Judy took over the operations of the farm. Plastic houses growing carnations and other cut flowers was what Ted had learned as part of his college education. So, it was natural that Ted was a successor giving Morizo and Emi their opportunity to retire.

## HONORS

*This photograph shows Morizo in back row, third from left, along with other agriculturalists honored by the Japanese Agriculture Society at the Consulate of Japan on December 18, 1972.*

*I found this slide of a trophy that was given to Morizo. Particulars are unknown.*

## SOME ASPECTS OF LIFE ON THE HOME FRONT TRAVELS

In their retirement years, Morizo and Emi traveled extensively. On several of those occasions, Grace and I took our kids with us to visit their home and sort of house-sit during their travels. We did this even before their retirement such as when they attended the Osaka World's Fair in 1964. Or, even before that when Morizo went to Japan to make Kyohei Murakami his adopted son to care for their Shiwa property.

Since coming to California in 1917, Morizo probably returned to Japan about five times. I recall that he returned to Japan to negotiate the adoption of Hirotoshi and later, Kyohei, to be caretakers and owners of the Shiwa properties. He also visited the Okabeppu family in Kagoshima in the 1960s. He also took Emi, my mother, and Tak, my brother, to see the Shiwa properties.

After all, he was a Japanese citizen, not an American citizen. It was not until 1952 that Japanese aliens could become qualified for American citizenship and pass the citizenship examination to be naturalized.

In hindsight, Grace and I have visited the Shiwa ancestral home more often than Morizo. We probably have a better perception than Morizo of the home before and after its improvements; but, we can never live in his footsteps.

I often fantasized about what would have happened if I had accepted a 1955 position with the Atomic Bomb Casualty Commission in Hiroshima, Japan, immediately after graduating from UCLA with my MBA degree, and moved to Hiroshima. Would I have managed and inherited the family homestead in Shiwa? If so, Morizo would not have had to adopt Kyohei as a son. What kind of situation would face the old homestead? Something to ponder.

From some of the slides and photographs that I have been able to procure, I can surmise that Morizo and Emi took several trips. Those pictures serve as a mild remembrance of their travels.

Regardless of where Morizo traveled, he managed to bring one small rock or pebble home on which he painted the dates of travel and location. Those rocks were put into a vat in the front entryway to the house. Those artifacts no longer exist among the siblings.

On some of their travels, Morizo and Emi befriended an Iwaki couple as well as Nemoto. So, some of the pictures show them along with Morizo and Emi.

*In this photograph, Morizo is in the center with Mr. Nemoto to the right.*
*He looks quite chipper.*
*I DO NOT KNOW THE REASON FOR MORIZO HAVING BANDAGE OR GAUZE ON HIS HEAD.*
*I do not recall the man at the left in the photograph.*

*Pictured are Iwaki and Morizo.*

Mr. and Mrs. Iwaki often traveled with Morizo and Emi on their Mexico and Latin American tours with travel agencies. I did not know much about the Iwaki family.

When Morizo and Emi wanted to go on tour, Grace and I, as much as possible, took vacation time from my administrative assignments so that they could travel.

Since we did not live with Morizo and Emi in retirement, my knowledge of their travels is quite limited.

## OKINAWA MURA

On one Latin American tour of Peru, Bolivia, Chile, Argentina, and Brazil, Morizo told me about the Okinawan tradition of New Year's Holiday.

The Okinawans established a fairly large village in Bolivia. Seven days of the New Year's holiday was celebrated with wives cooking seven days of food for the family. Then, the wives slipped out and gallivanted wherever they pleased, either with friends or visited places, or stayed with others. Who knows what they did, but it was their freedom.

Among many of us, including Morizo, it was common for the men to visit various people for some food and liquor while the wives stayed home to welcome guests . . . quite the opposite of what happened in Okinawa Mura.

For Morizo, the celebration of the New Year was not a big deal because he was not much of a drinker. One gulp of sake or wine made his face beet red and he was done . . . no more drinking. I know that I did not inherit any of this trait from Morizo because I am a good drinker of fine liquors.

*Morizo with fishing pole.*

## FISHING WITH BILL YOKOYAMA

No longer having Yutaka to urge Morizo to go fishing, at times, he took up with Bill Yokoyama who fished out of San Diego on extra day excursions. Bill belonged to a Nikkei fishing club in Orange County and so, often went fishing with members of the club. But, on some occasions, Morizo joined Bill in his fishing venture.

Deep-sea fishing was not for me. When I looked beyond the horizon on a boat, I was a goner . . . vomit, queasy stomach.

## IWAKI AND MORIZO

*I found several pictures that seemed to feature a visit to Latin American countries. I have included them here to show that they enjoyed their retirement years in travel.*

The Morizo Story

Jack Fujimoto

I knew that my parents traveled to Europe with tour groups and also took some cruises. I could not find many pictures of these travels.

The Morizo Story

Jack Fujimoto

## SOME ASPECTS OF LIFE ON THE HOME FRONT

Generally speaking, Morizo and Emi, in their retirement years, spent life at their home, interspersed with an occasional visit by some friends or their offsprings.

*Pictured is Morizo eating a slice of watermelon in front of the farmhouse.*

Morizo took several breaks during his working days to eat fruit while Emi observed. In Jolene's paper for her class at UCLA Asian Studies, this type of photograph is appropriate in that despite all of their hardships, *baachan* thought that *jiichan* was an ideal mate.

*Morizo and Emi with Randall Fujimoto, grandson.*

Randall, at times, played Morizo's favorite games of blackjack and solitaire. He had a close relationship with *Jiichan* (grandfather) and *Baachan* (grandmother).

The Morizo Story

*Morizo is being checked by Victor Fujimoto, son of Archie and grandson of Yutaka Fujimoto.*

Even at a young age, Victor came to the house to talk to *Jiichan* and *Baachan*, who treated Victor as one of the family.

Victor is currently a professor of medicine at UCSF (University of California at San Francisco).

*Morizo and Emi (jiichan and baachan) are seated next to their great-grandchildren, four generations through Fumi, Dawna, and the two, Marissa and Misty.*

Both grandchildren, as of this writing are proud mothers of families of their own as well as working to make their American dreams come true.

Misty is currently a medical doctor in psychiatry for pediatrics at UCLA.

*Morizo at his workbench trimming his bonsai plants.*

## VISITS

*Pictured are Archie, Otowa, Morizo, and Kaneto.*

In retirement, there were occasional visits. One such memorable visit was Kaneto Shindo and his wife, Nobuko Otowa, the noted

Japanese Lenin Peace Prize film director and Otowa, the noted actress famous for Tojin Okichi series of Japanese drama. Grace and I saw them a few times when we visited Japan.

Kaneto and Nobuko visited the farm to chat with Morizo and Emi. On two occasions, they came to Southern California to view the landscape with Archie and eventually took shots of Imperial Valley as well as San Diego areas. It was Archie who showed them around.

Kaneto produced the romance of Archie and Keiko. *Sekai no Hana Yome* was a title that I recalled he made.

*Pictured is my brother, Tak, walking his dog in Morizo's homestead in Encinitas.*

Kaneto, being a world renown cinematographer, writer, director, and producer once invited my brother, Tak, who is in the movie industry, to visit Japan, but I do not think that the invitation panned out.

Jack Fujimoto

*Poster board says, "Hiroshima is my town."*

In any event, we visited Kaneto when his 100th birthday was being celebrated in Hiroshima with his directing a film.

*One of the rare photographs of mochi tsuki (pounding of mochi rice) for the traditional New Year's celebration. Hajime Matsumoto of Solana Beach (Ted's father) used his garage for the several families to bring their rice, process it through swinging of the mallet and the making of traditional rice cakes, and in the process have delicious food with friends.*

## INVESTMENTS
## CAPITAL FUNDS

When Morizo had to get into the flower business, he had to expend considerable capital to build plastic enclosed hothouses.

Carnations were grown in these sheltered wooden-framed enclosures. Sprinklers and fertilization systems were put into place. Ventilation had to be provided. So, all of these capital improvements required a considerable outlay of funds.

As I did his annual income tax filings, I recognized that Morizo had revenue that he could invest in the stock market. I noticed that he did stock transactions with Los Angeles-based securities firms such as Nomura and Taiyo Tamazuka.

From his income tax filings, there were not large capital gains. On the contrary, the brokers tended to push (IPO) Initial Public Offerings in new ventures. Some questionable ones involved mining stocks in Mexico or the Canadian exchanges.

With his limited command of the English language, I tended to feel that he got into stocks that were translated into the Japanese language.

In general, Morizo was a successful investor of personal funds.

## PARTING

Emi passed away on June 2, 1989, at the age of eighty-two.

Morizo passed away on May 30, 1994, at the age of ninety-two.

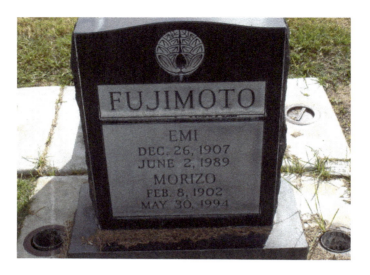

One headstone in Mount Hope Cemetery, San Diego, has ashes of both. Also, ashes of Morizo and Emi are in the Shiwa family generational headstone (代々の墓). Only Emi's ashes are in the Kubo cemetery in Yasuno mura in Hiroshima.

# MORIZO IN HIS LATER YEARS

Emi passed away in 1989.

Morizo would often say that his circle of acquaintances was getting smaller and therefore, he openly said and became quite lonely. No Iwaki. No Nemoto. Archie was still around to converse and discuss matters with him.

I did not visit much inasmuch as I was involved in work as chairman of the board of Trustees of the Institute of Buddhist Studies (IBS) in Berkeley, California, and at the same time, president of Los Angeles Mission College in Sylmar (San Fernando Valley).

The farmhouse went through a remodel in 1992.

From the time that Emi passed away in 1989 and Morizo's expiring in 1994, a five-year span, Fumie spent some time living at the farmhouse and cared for his welfare.

She wrote that Morizo spent days playing solitaire in his favorite spot outdoors on the west side of the farmhouse. When his grandkids visited, it was often playing blackjack with them using his old crinkled cards.

In the afternoon, Morizo sat under the tree in front of the garage looking for the mailman to come. Since he invested with some Los Angeles-based brokers, he got several financial reports. He also read the *Rafu Shimpo*, a Los Angeles-based Japanese language newspaper.

At mealtime, he sat in the kitchen where he had a chair and access to a table with a toaster oven, a rice cooker filled with rice, and a bowl of *tsukemono* (pickled vegetables) and pot of tea. Often, what he ate was *ochazuke* (just a bowl of rice with tea poured on it and eaten with pickled vegetables as a condiment). He was content with that.

Morizo, according to Fumie, really liked to go out and be treated to a fast-food milk shake. At home, he occasionally drank coffee with lots of sugar and milk. At night, he settled for his Twinkies (sort of a cream-filled éclair).

## POTPOURRI

*Pictured is Jack under the wisteria tree where Morizo sat for hours on end to watch the mailman deliver the mail, so that he could rush and get it.*

## 1992 HOUSE REMODEL

*Pictured is baachan with some of her grandchildren as they witness the remodeling of the old house built in 1948.*

*View from the south side.*

*View of original sheds for tractor, equipment, and fertilizers that was not affected by the 1992 remodel.*

*Northside view of the house as the remodel takes place.*

# MORIZO'S SIBLINGS

## MORIZO'S OLDEST SISTER, TAZUNO

Tazuno was born in 1888, fourteen years older than Morizo. Through my contact with her one daughter, Yoshiye, I learned that her father, Tajima, worked for a public utilities firm in Hiroshima Prefecture.

Even though we often visited the Shiwa homestead, Yoshiye very seldom talked about her mother and therefore never gathered any intelligence on Toshiye.

*Pictured are Yoshiye and adopted son, Akihiko.*

Yoshiye was grateful to Morizo as she told me about his giving her a home where she could live with her adopted son. The home was adjacent to the home occupied by Kyohei and Nobuko Fujimoto, along with her three sons (fourth son drowned in a pond).

Akihiko was seldom home when we visited Nobuko Fujimoto at the homestead. Yoshiye visited and often stayed. Akihiko was in Thailand most of the time according to Yoshiye.

Jack Fujimoto

## SHIZUNO, SECOND IN LINE OF BIRTH

Shizuno was born in 1890. Married to Zentaro Imada and had one child, Hajime, who died in three days. The couple later divorced.

She married Toragesa Okabeppu. Shizuno died at sixty-seven years of age. She is featured prominently in the Yasukichi side of the Fujimoto family.

Shizuno was twelve years older than Morizo. She gave birth to six children who in turn led to another twenty grandchildren.

*Pictured are Akira Okabeppu on the left, two males who I assume are husbands of Toshiye Okabeppu and Meriko Okabeppu.*
*Brothers, Itaru, Hayato, and Takeshi are not pictured here.*

## SAYO, THIRD IN LINE OF BIRTH

Sayo was born in 1893, nine years older than Morizo. After divorcing her first husband, Zentaro Takaoka, she married Yoshitaka

Utada, a taxi firm operator in Hiroshima. I learned that he was well-to-do having a fleet of cabs.

She had four boys, all of whom served in the Japanese military war effort during World War II. I was told that one was a kamikaze pilot. Only one of the brothers survived the war. I never got to meet him.

Sayo also had two daughters, Tomiko and Teruko, both of whom Grace and I got to know well during our many visits to Japan. Both had colorful stories to tell about their war experiences.

*Pictured below are members of the Utada family. Names of the boys, I do not know. The daughters are Teruko on the left and Tomiko on the right.*

## YUTAKA, FOURTH IN LINE OF BIRTH

Yutaka was born in 1896, six years older than Morizo. Much has already been written about Yutaka in foregoing pages. Yutaka died at fifty-one years of age in La Jolla, California, from an accident.

Jack Fujimoto

## YAYA, FIFTH IN LINE OF BIRTH

I could not find much about Yaya. She is listed as born in 1898. She married Ginzaburo Okabeppu, brother to Toragesa.

The Morizo Story

*Pictured are Mataichi Murakami, Kisano Fujimoto, and their son, Choji.*

## KISANO, SIXTH IN LINE OF BIRTH

Kisano is listed as born in 1900. Kisano is only two years older than Morizo but seemed to be in close correspondence with Morizo. When the issue of the property rights to the Shiwa homestead came up after Yutaka met an untimely death, it was Kisano's grandson mentioned as landowner. When the older grandson, Hirotoshi, took responsibility for a while but abdicated to go to work for TOTO, Morizo asked Kyohei Murakami to be his adopted son and thus, landowner. Kyohei accepted.

Kisano married Mataichi Murakami, who eventually became chief of police for the major city, Hiroshima. It was an awesome responsibility.

During World War II, Mataichi Murakami died in New Guinea according to his son.

Jack Fujimoto

## MORIZO, SEVENTH IN LINE OF BIRTH

Morizo was born in 1902.

## SAYOKO, EIGHTH IN LINE OF BIRTH

Records show that Sayoko was born 1904 and died in 1907.

*Yasuko is pictured with Kyohei, Morizo's adopted son.*

## YASUKO, NINTH IN LINE OF BIRTH

Yasuko was born in 1906. She was a colorful lady. When Grace and I visited Japan, which we often did, she related some interesting tales.

One story that she told me was that when she left school, she sought a job as a detective in Tokyo. It was unheard of at the time, but she sought the job to establish a precedent for women as well as seek a male companion. She said that she did not stay long on that job.

Another story was that a widower whom Morizo knows well asked Yasuko if she wanted to marry him. She got divorced from her partner in Tanegashima, an island south of Kagoshima, and told this widower "No, thanks." Reason was that his *doogu* (penis) was valueless. Interesting story.

*Pictured are Yasuko and her husband.*

The couple ran a small country market on the island, Tanegashima.

# MORIZO'S LEGACY ALBUM

This album of photographs further the legacy of Morizo and Emi. Photographs are scarce. Captioning is more extensive to extend the legacy.

*Morizo and Emi in one of their rare poses.*

The picture of Morizo and Emi above appears to be taken in the backyard of the house where Morizo made a pond similar to the one that Yutaka made in Poston camp. He grew rare tropical fruit such as sapota, cherimoya, guava, and other exotics from Ito nursery in Leucadia.

Jack Fujimoto

*This is a rare photograph showing Morizo and Emi with their children as well as grandchildren.
Probably taken in the 1970s.*

## VISIT TO JAPAN

*Pictured from left are Tomiko Shimizu, Morizo, and Kaneto Shindo.*

Taken in 1960s during one of his rare visits to Japan. Tomiko is eldest in Morizo's older sister, Sayo Utada's family and married to

Sempa Shimizu, noted Japanese airplane pilot. There are several books written in Japanese that feature the work done by Sempa Shimizu. I read in one of the books that Sempa was delivering a plane from Japan to the heartland of America when he ran out of fuel on the island of Maui, one of the Hawaiian islands.

I was personally proud over the fact that I could still read the Japanese language books.

Kaneto Shindo is world-renown film producer, director, and writer. His sister, Hisayo, is wife of Morizo's older brother, Yutaka. Hisayo, I understand, never returned to her Hiroshima roots after marrying Yutaka. She wrote letters to her brother and others which Kaneto later produced as a documentary featured on NHK (Nippon Hoso Kyoku) titled *CHIHEISEN* (Horizon).

*Pictured are Emi's cousins in Hiroshima, Makoto Kubo, and Itsuye Nakano.*

I took *this* photograph in 2010 when we visited them as sort of a reunion, sushi, sake, and dessert cakes at Makoto's home.

Makoto and his wife, Fumi, live in retirement from shiitake mushroom growing on a hill overlooking a valley with a beautiful view. It is the same hill that Emi, her brother, Goso, and younger sister, Hozumi, lived and went to elementary school.

Itsuye Nakano is Emi's cousin being Itsuye Yoneda. Her brothers were Hitoshi Frank Yoneda and John Narumi Yoneda, both being Kibei Nisei (second generation immigrant children who went to Japan and returned to the USA). Both Frank and John faced discriminatory practices in the workplace during the 1930s.

## ARCHIE

Archie Fujimoto was of immeasurable help to Morizo and Emi in their retirement days. Despite his busy schedule with his mother, Hisayo's needs, and Morizo asking for favors, Archie was like a good-humored man, doing tasks in good spirits.

In my estimation, Archie was more of a son than me. He lived nearby and was involved with the Nikkei culture of the greater San Diego region. Families called Archie to repair their Homecast Japanese language radio broadcasts and later, their reception of Japanese language television broadcasts. Archie was very knowledgeable in electronics as I knew growing up with him in our formative years.

In the early 1930s, Archie ordered electronics kits to build radios, shortwave radio, Morse code tapping equipment, and other gadgets. In Poston concentration camp, he would team with Sam Goda to pursue electronics interests.

World War II and the loyalty questionnaire administered in Poston camp caused some hardship inasmuch as he was stripped of his birthplace citizenship and placed in a US Department of Justice facility in Santa Fe, New Mexico. He was scheduled to go to Japan because of his citizenship status, but he declined: no food in a defeated nation, no shelter unless he went to live with grandfather Yasukichi, and never visited Japan. By the time in 1946 or 1947, the concentration camps were closed and Archie had to get his citizenship back, he finally emerged to live a "new life." This would lead to his becoming the head of the Yutaka household when Yutaka had an accident working for Ben Vau and expired.

Since then, Archie was a tremendous help to his mother as well as to Morizo and Emi.

## MORIZO IN A NAME

*Stuart and Maya Ida family with Jaxon and Tess.*

Maya is Morizo's granddaughter. Their son is named Jaxon Morizo Ida. The Morizo legacy continues with great-grandchildren being a name carrier.

*Pictured is the Gerald and Jolene Morita family with children, Matthew (MJ) and Hailey (HK).*
*MJ is named Matthew Jameson Morizo Morita.*
*The influence of Morizo is felt among the fourth generation of Morita families.*

## FAMILY LIFE

*Pictured are the Jack and Grace Fujimoto family of Crystal, Maya, Jolene, and Randall. Taken in 1960s. They are third generation from Morizo and Emi.*

*Pictured are Emi with youngest daughter, Eiko.*

After Eiko retired, she went to the farmhouse to help with some flower growing and making dried flowers to help Morizo and Emi with their busy flower growing experiences. She enjoyed it greatly, especially the dried flowers which to this day still adorn the living rooms of friends.

*Pictured are Tomi Yokoyama, Emi, Judy, and Hozumi Kawamoto.*

Hozumi Kawamoto is younger sister to Emi.

Judy is the fifth child among the six children to be born to Emi.

Tomiko Yokoyama is the wife of George Yokoyama who was at a banquet for the Yokoyama family.

In the old Yoneda homestead in Yasuno Mura in Hiroshima, the Yokoyama house was adjacent to where Emi spent about ten years going to school and working in an office.

*Pictured are Emi, Morizo, Jack and Grace.*

Our family tradition featuring the birthday of someone reaching the age of sixty gets to wear a red cap and red garb, basically, to start a new life cycle of sixty years. It was my turn to wear the red cap, but suffice it to say that the usual gifts of money wrapped in red did not flow my way. Anyway, it was a fun-filled evening of tasty Chinese food at a local restaurant.

*Pictured is Morizo blowing out candles from his birthday cake.*

The Morizo Story

*Morizo and Emi are at restaurant featuring Chinese food with the Yokoyama Family.*
*Identified left to right are Harry with wife, Bob, Tomiko and George, Bill and Haru, and Kazuko with Frank.*

*This is an early picture of Frank Hitoshi Yoneda.*
*His wife, Hatsuye Hatakeda, is to his right.*
*His two boys, Bobby and Denny, are in front.*
*The picture appears to have been taken in front of the Emperor's moat in Tokyo.*
*Frank is cousin to Emi.*

*Pictured are Emi and Morizo on the road to Death Valley National Monument.*

Morizo was a farmer, his clothes were casual, and it did not seem to faze him how he looked. Emi was conscious of clothes because women in the family talked about clothes. Besides, Emi knew how to sew, having made dresses for the girls.

*Emi's brother, Karl Goso Yoneda, is flanked by his cousin, John Narumi Yoneda, and his wife, Sue Hatsuye Osaki Yoneda.*

# ACKNOWLEDGEMENTS

If Morizo and Emi followed typical Japanese tradition, I, as the oldest son, would have been expected to follow in their footsteps and become a farmer. But, being in America, and living through California's anti-Japanese discriminatory laws and practices and wanting to send me to Japan prior to the Pacific War, Morizo liberated me to pursue my education after graduating from San Dieguito High School in Encinitas, California.

I am grateful to Morizo for that decision. That decision opened the door to my being able to pursue my education and dreams of making a difference in America's higher education circles, be it in the classroom, teaching online, developing new college curricula, back-to-basics educational systems, or in the college president's chair for twenty years.

Sorry, Morizo and Emi, that I could not showcase more photographs of your life together for sixty-two years. I suspect that most of the picture albums and individual photographs got lost when the house was expanded and remodeled.

I recall sending many pictures of the atomic bomb blast on Hiroshima that were taken on that day. My friend in my army

Jack Fujimoto

unit in Kobe, Japan, gave me that treasure which I sent home for Morizo and Emi to see and keep. But, they could not be located.

Also, I looked for one particular picture which I wanted to showcase. I was especially fond of the breakfast nook that I made during my break from college. It had an odd-shaped table, where Morizo sat with his *chazuke* (rice with tea and pickles) and at night, with his milk and sweets (usually Twinkies or sweet roll). That nook also housed the rice that was used for the family meal. I looked through our limited photograph collection and could not find it. Sorry, because that one photograph would open additional stories.

I thank all of siblings as well as the extended family for their additions to *The Morizo Story*, mostly in the form of comments to notes that my son, Randall, put together that were sent to them in book form.

I thank my sister Judy and her daughter Tam for keeping me informed of Morizo and Emi in Amida land. During this period of my life where we have a global pandemic, I was told that Morizo and Emi are visiting each of their children in our earthly pursuits. Emi is the pretty yellow butterfly that I see in our backyard often. It is gratifying that the link continues.

In 2021, I am indirectly thankful to the global pandemic that forced me to confront my physical deterioration and spring forward to finish *The Morizo Story* to its conclusion in print. Contact with Emily Perkins of FriesenPress is making this conclusion possible.

I entered hospice care on September 1, 2020 and am grateful that a team of medical personnel look after my basic needs. I also get help from a team of palliative care funded staff through Keiro Services. All support for me who suffers from IPF and Grace with her MCI are most grateful.

To my wife, Grace Fusaye Toya Fujimoto, our children, Crystal Sanae, Randall Tadao, Jolene Emi, and April Maya, I owe and

The Morizo Story

greatly appreciate their support in concluding a milestone in my life . . . painting a tribute to Morizo.

Much of this biography was written in notes but with the specter of the USA COVID-19, I hastily finished its writing. So, many errors, omissions, and memory recall deficiencies are mine for which I take responsibility.

Masakazu Jack Fujimoto, Ph.D.

*Pictured with my hat and nasal cannula tubes.*

CPSIA information can be obtained
at www.ICGtesting.com
Printed in the USA
BVHW090610221221
624594BV00019B/1767